NO MORE

HOPE FOR AN OUT-OF-CONTROL MOM

MORE

ANGER

ENDORSEMENTS

The title promises *No More Anger* but child abuse is merely an example of the struggles each of us face. Kathy Collard Miller's memoir is a revealing look at problems that are rooted in bitterness, hypocrisy that prevents us from seeking help, and a self-focus that blinds us from seeing the big picture. While Kathy honestly shares her desperation, she also gives us a roadmap to victory so we can find release from the problem that grips us. *No More Anger* reads like a novel but has the weight of a theology course. I couldn't put it down.

—**Roxann Andersen**, co-author, *The Marriage Dance*, www. TheMarriageDance.com, www.Facebook.com/themarriagedance

No More Anger is an intensely candid, unsanitized account of God's help in one woman's struggle against anger through faith and diligence, learning how to surrender to, and work with God. As exceedingly difficult parts of the book were to read, especially knowing the story is non-fiction, I was compelled to read the entire book in one sitting. Kathy Collard Miller's gambit of emotions are excellently communicated allowing anyone else who struggles with anger to the point of abuse, the freedom to seek help with genuine hope for resolution. Her story is a wonderful testimony of God's love transcending our behavior and being the only possible source for transformation.

—**Rev. Pamela Christian**, International Minister, Speaker, Author and Media Host

Kathy gives her readers a riveting ride through the struggle to get free of uncontrollable rage and hurting her precious daughter. Her testimony of opening up to another mom gives us all hope in practicing transparency in biblical community. I was moved to tears more than once as she beautifully unfolded the healing and redemption found in the unconditional love of our God. Kathy shares several practical guidelines and truths God gave to walk her out of her deep pain and abusive patterns. This is a must read for any raging momma.

—**Roxanna Grimes**, author of *Pearl: The Art of Being Found Loved and Valued in the Heart of God*

Written in a journal format, the reader gets a glimpse behind closed doors of the frustration, guilt, anger and raw, honest emotions this young mother hid from her family, her church and her friends. It is a 'no holds barred' compelling story which builds momentum to the point when suicide seemed like the only answer to stop Kathy Collard Miller from physically and emotionally abusing her little girl. No matter what type of anger or frustration we have to struggle with, the author paints a clear picture of how our faith in God is the answer to anything we need to overcome.

—**Carol Graham**, Author of *Battered Hope* and show host for *Never Ever Giving Up Hope*

Tears, shock, sorrow, and compassion explode inside with each scene of *No More Anger*. As the pages read like a riveting novel, the reader walks with the author through the pain of sin but continues on to confession, faith, commitment, and beautiful victory.

This is a must read for any mom caught in the snare of insecurity—for every young husband to reveal the importance of understanding. *No More Anger* is also a must read for any young wife contemplating motherhood. I cheered the victory and was moved by God's everlasting love, His grace and mercy.—**Janet Perez Eckles**, international speaker and author

KATHY
COLLARD
MILLER

NO MORE

HOPE FOR AN OUT-OF-CONTROL MOM

ANGER

Elk Lake
PUBLISHING, INC.
35 Dogwood Drive
Plymouth, MA 02360

Library Cataloging Data
Names: Miller, Kathy Collard (Kathy Collard Miller)
No More Anger: Hope for an Out-of-Control Mom / Kathy Collard Miller
184 p. 23cm × 15cm (9in × 6 in.)
Description: For years, Kathy Collard Miller battled with anger that had, on occasion, led to her abusing her beloved daughter. But in the midst of all her pain, she found hope.
Identifiers: ISBN-13: 978-46638-56-4 (trade) | 978-1-946638-57-1 (POD) | 978-1-946638-58-81 (e-book)
Key Words: Abuse, Parenting, Children, Relationships, Family, Jesus, Faith
LCCN: 2017962814 Nonfiction

DEDICATION

To my wonderful daughter, Darcy,
who graciously allows our story to be shared for God's glory.

TABLE OF CONTENTS

FOREWORD

Her voice was high-pitched. "Jackson, I told you not to walk next to the fire pit unless a grownup is with you. You could get burned!" I watched as the almost three-year-old looked directly at his mother, smiled broadly, and intentionally put one foot over an imaginary line, which placed him even closer to potential danger.

The exhausted young mama ran to his side and yelled, "You are in 'time out' right now, young man!" She grabbed him by the arm, stormed into the house, and slammed him into a chair. "If you *dare* to move before I finish counting to twenty-five, you are getting a spanking. DO YOU UNDERSTAND?"

Julie (not her real name) was in my Bible study, and I sensed the frustration of a weary mother who was trying to balance a full-time, demanding job with being the mother of a precocious, energetic preschooler who tested the limits of his parents multiple times a day. She looked at me and said, "I can't wait for the weekend to be over so I can go back to work. I'm a terrible mother! I yell and scream and make threats that Jackson can't even understand."

Over time, she told me she had trouble controlling her anger when her son was strong-willed and difficult. Jackson knew exactly how to get on her last nerve and delighted in pushing her into a frenzy of frustration. Life got even more complicated when Lucas, her husband, had multiple out-of-town business trips that took him away for two and three days at a time. He came home and got to be "the fun parent," and Julie always seemed to get stuck with keeping routines intact and with handling all of the discipline. Julie resented this and often begged Lucas to help, but he would laugh off her comments and play hard with Jackson right before bedtime, leaving Julie with the task of quieting him down and putting him to bed, which often took up to an hour. Julie told me she resented her husband for not sharing in the difficult parenting responsibilities and with leaving her with more than she felt capable of handling.

Whether or not you identify with the frustration Julie experienced, every person struggles with anger to some degree. And regardless, the book you are holding will inspire you to know God wants to help you in whatever struggle seems hopeless or difficult.

In Kathy Collard Miller's memoir, *No More Anger*, you'll not only identify with her personal experience of feeling like an out-of-control mom, you'll understand the thin line between appropriate discipline and child abuse. Kathy's vulnerability about her long and arduous journey to becoming a better mother and learning how to control her anger will give you renewed hope, fresh courage, and a plan of action to turn your overwhelming irritation and raw emotions into a fresh beginning.

Kathy reminds all of us that when we stay isolated and don't share our internal pain and wrong choices with anyone, we feel completely alone and unable to cope. Her story will breathe new life into your exhausted spirit. This powerful book includes important questions for every chapter. It will allow you to honestly explore what's happened in your life that influences the way you parent your child—and it will reveal important strategies for coming out of chaos and learning a different and better way to manage your erratic emotions.

If you want to learn how to control your anger and respond differently to the stresses of marriage and parenting, read this book. I'm grateful to Kathy for vulnerably telling her story in a way that gives you and me the chance to say: "I've been there. I'm there now. I want to change with God's help." This is a book that could change your life for the better and it's a resource you'll want to give to other people.

—**Carol Kent**, Speaker and Author, *He Holds My Hand: Experiencing God's Presence & Protection* (Tyndale)

CHAPTER 1

ANGER CONTROLLED ME

March 1, 1977

Two-year-old, blonde-headed Darcy splashed in the bathtub amid suds and toys.

"Time to wash your hair," I announced.

"No, no, Mommy. No wash hair. Please."

"Oh yes. It's all sticky. It'll feel good to get it nice and clean," I coaxed.

Darcy broke into tears as I rubbed the shampoo into her hair. Suddenly she yelled, "It's in my eyes. It hurts! It hurts!"

"Oh, it is not." Annoyance began a slow burn within me. *Here she goes again! She does this every single time. I just hate it!* "There're no suds near your eyes. Besides, it's baby shampoo—it doesn't sting."

She screamed louder. Without warning, I was engulfed with exhaustion. The pressures mounting throughout the day overwhelmed me and I felt weak. The room seemed to close in on me. The dampness and heat made my clothes stick to my skin.

Pushing limp hair away from my forehead and gritting my teeth, I hissed back, "Darcy, there's no shampoo in your eyes! Now hold still or you're in big trouble! Hold still, I said!"

Shrieking, she clawed at her eyes. I turned on the faucet and jerked her to it, pushing her whole head under the running water. Soap flowed down over her face into the tub. She sputtered and coughed, but I didn't care. She was going to get clean whether she liked it or not.

I hurriedly turned off the water. Grabbing her arm, I yanked her out of the tub. Darcy stood shivering and crying. I screamed at her again and again. "The next time you'll hold still when I tell you. We'll do it the way I say and that's that."

I felt like an erupting volcano of hate. Anger and frustration boiled inside me like hot lava. At that moment I felt like I wanted to get rid of the problem—her.

Spanking her with my hand found an outlet for my tension and exhaustion. But spanking became uncontrolled beating, until Darcy's hysterical shrieking brought me back to reason. I carried her into her room and dropped her onto the bed. Slamming the door behind me, I bolted down the hall sobbing.

"Oh, Lord Jesus," I gasped. "I hurt Darcy again. I keep saying I won't do it anymore, but I can't control my anger. What's wrong with me?"

I knelt beside my bed and cried for a long time. Darcy's muffled cries reached me, suffocating me in a blanket of guilt.

My thoughts hurled through my mind like hailstones in a storm. *I've been a Christian for ten years; how can I be so angry? I lead a Bible study and other people think I'm a strong Christian; how can I be acting like this?*

I wanted to scream, "Help me! Help me!" but I was ashamed and frightened. *What if they take my kids away from me? What if everyone knows I abuse my child?*

"I'm not a child abuser," I whispered. "Or am I? I'm still hurting her," I cried out. "I'm *abusing* my own child. Oh, God, no." The word abusing echoed through my mind like a boulder thudding down a canyon wall—strong and final. There was no hope. I had prayed; I had cried; I had begged for deliverance. If only Larry didn't have to work at night, he could relieve some of the pressure.

I can't tell him, he's a cop. He arrests people who do this. Would he arrest me? How long can I continue like this without seriously injuring Darcy or baby Mark?

Darcy's frightened face flashed before me, wrenching my heart like a tree being uprooted by the wind. *I don't want to hurt them. I love them. I want to be the best mother in the world. But I'm so far from that.*

"Oh, Father," I whimpered. "Help me. You've got to. I can't help myself."

I turned my attention to Darcy and couldn't hear her crying anymore. Walking quietly to her room, I opened the door and peeked in. Her naked body huddled by the pillow up against the wall. She saw me and started crying again. Pushing aside my shame, I pulled her pajamas out of her drawer and started to dress her. Her body grew tense at my touch.

"Don't be afraid, Darcy," I murmured, trying to push back tears begging to cascade my cheeks from the back of my eyes. "I'm not mad at you anymore. Mommy was wrong to hurt you. I'm sorry. I wish I could promise you I'm never going to get angry with you again but I can't. Oh, how I wish I could." My tears finally gushed out and then plopped onto the sheets beside her. I gently tucked her into bed and left the room.

As I put on my nightgown, I wondered, *God, do you care? Have you deserted me?*

Of course not, Kathy, I chided myself. *You know better than that. God is always there.*

Then where is the help I need? I wanted to shout. But I pushed the doubt out of my mind as I cried myself to sleep.

CHAPTER 2
PROMISES! PROMISES!

March 10

Ignoring Thursday and Friday as they passed, I clung to one anchoring thought of sanity: Saturday would be here soon. Larry had agreed to take care of Darcy and Mark so I could go clothes shopping. The thought of being out in the real world all by myself for the first time since Mark was born three months ago excited me.

Saturday morning finally arrived. As I survived Darcy's temper tantrum at the breakfast table and Mark's dirty diaper, I looked forward to those few hours of peace and quiet while browsing in the mall. Even though several stubborn pounds refused to yield after my pregnancy, I wanted to find a new outfit to enhance my appearance and boost my spirits.

By the time Larry sleepily walked into the kitchen around ten o'clock, I had verified the checkbook's presence in my purse two different times.

"Good morning, sweetheart," I joyfully greeted him. "You look rested. Your breakfast is on the table and the kids are clean and happy. I'm hoping I'll be back by lunchtime."

Larry's baffled look set off warning bells in my mind. "Where are you going?"

"Don't you remember? You said I could go clothes shopping today."

"Oh," he muttered. "I forgot. In fact, I don't really remember saying that at all."

"But, honey, you said on Monday Saturday would be a good day for you to take care of the kids."

He still looked bewildered. "I'm sorry, Kathy, but I told Ken we would fly to San Diego today. He's wanted me to take him for a long time, and today's the only day he can go. And the Cessna I've been wanting to try out is available at the flying club. I guess you'll just have to go another time."

My throat tensed with disappointment. Despairing thoughts jumbled my words. "But, Larry, you promised. I've been waiting all week for today. I've just got to get out for a while. You don't know what it's like ..."

"Well, I'm really sorry, but I promised Ken. You can go shopping any time."

Any time. Oh, sure, any time, except when you're flying or when you're working your part-time second job in real estate or when you need to sleep ten hours a day. Right, any time.

Angry tears clouded my vision as I furiously wiped the counter. I knew from experience no matter how long I might debate, the case was closed.

Thirty minutes later when Larry kissed Darcy good-bye, the tenseness in my throat crept into my neck. I followed him down the hall, trying to find the right words which would make him see reason and know my pain. Seeing him shut the door of the laundry room behind him which led into the garage, I wanted to scream, "Don't slam the door in my face as if I'm nothing. You can't even say goodbye? Am I that disgusting to you?"

My rage surfaced in sobs and cursing. I choked on the apple I was eating and in my fury, hurled it at the door. It shattered as it hit the door and little bits of white apple pieces splattered onto the walls and ceiling of the laundry room. The apple core fell to the floor.

"Larry," I shouted, "I hate you! I hate you! Can't you see our relationship is dying? Sometimes I wish you wouldn't come back. Your plane can crash for all I care."

Frantically, I stumbled to my bed, knelt on the floor, clasping my hands together. "God, go ahead. Make his plane crash. I'll be better off."

I imagined the scene of Larry's funeral, friends and relatives telling me how brave I am to be so strong. They don't know I am delighted about his death. I'm free!

"Mommy, Mommy, cartoons over." Darcy's announcement snapped me out of my self-indulgent reverie, and I slowly pushed myself up knowing Larry's dirty breakfast dishes and Mark's hungry cry awaited me.

As I walked past the laundry room, I reached over and picked up the apple core. Staring at the apple pieces adhered to the walls and ceiling, I bitterly thought, "Those shattered apple pieces are just like my marriage, shattered. Just as no one can put this apple together, no one can put this broken marriage together. Not even you, God." I resisted raising my fist in defiance to God, but if he had appeared in human form in front of me, I would tell him, "You are a powerless God. Just try to bring us together. You can't do it." As I walked toward the kitchen, I felt triumphant knowing for once I was right. *There is no hope. Larry will never change. But if he would, then I can become the woman and wife God wants me to be. Good luck with that, God.*

When Larry returned in the evening, Darcy's excited greeting drowned my silence. After tucking the kids into bed, I told Larry goodnight. "How come you're going to bed so early?"

"I don't feel well. It was a rough day." I hoped he wouldn't press me further. I didn't even want to talk to him.

"All right. I hope you feel better tomorrow. Good night."

Lying motionless in bed as tears trickled down my cheeks and onto my pillow, I wanted to scream my pain at him. *If you really love me, spend more time with me. Choose me instead of everything else you do.* Then I rebuked myself. *That sounds so selfish. I can't say that.* But the feeling I wasn't first in his life continued to chip away at the foundation of our marriage.

Later, when he gently pulled the covers back and slowly slipped into bed, I pretended to be asleep. It wasn't until I heard his steady, deep breathing I finally relaxed and fell asleep.

For the next couple of days I struggled to blow out the flame of my anger and bitterness. But like a trick birthday candle, it rekindled each time I thought about Larry's insensitivity toward my needs. I felt depressed and helpless, as if I were riding a raft down a coursing river, without oars or a rope. And my distress calls to God seemed unheard.

On Tuesday afternoon after Larry left for work, I loaded the kids into the car and headed to visit my friend Jill. She greeted me at her door, casually dressed in worn jeans and a green turtleneck sweater. Her red-haired, eighteen-month-old son, Aaron, toddled after her.

We settled comfortably onto her newly upholstered plaid couch to watch the news on TV and chat. Aaron and Darcy sat on the floor and scribbled with their crayons as Mark lay on my lap chewing on a rattle. After a while, the newscaster related a story about a couple who had been arrested for child abuse. My heart started pounding and I took a deep breath.

"You know, Jill, sometimes I understand how parents might be tempted to mistreat their children. Kids sure can make parents angry." Laughing nervously, I looked at her and hesitantly waited for her reaction.

"Well, I sure can't," she retorted, shaking her head. "Those people are awful. They ought to be arrested."

I jerked my head away, hot tears stinging my eyes. *Lord, am I really that bad? Doesn't anyone else get angry like I do?*

Gratefully, I heard Jill's phone ring. While she was gone, I wiped away my tears. *I'm never going to let anyone know how angry I can become.*

Later when I drove home, I concluded, *I must not be allowing God to help me in some way. But what is it?*

Maybe I'm not praying enough! In an attempt to change, I affirmed my commitment out loud, "Lord, I promise to pray more every day." Yet, I knew my vows had been ineffective in the past. A seed of doubt sprouted within me.

CHAPTER 3

IN TRAINING

March 20

Darcy's training pants were wet again. Again. *I can't believe it. She messed them only forty-five minutes ago. She promised she would tell me the next time she needed to go.*

Marching over to her, I pushed her into the bathroom. I struggled to pull down the soaking pants. *What am I doing wrong? She's never going to learn.*

"Darcy, you're supposed to come into the bathroom and use the potty chair. Remember you promised Mommy you would go in the potty chair. Why can't you learn?"

She's doing it on purpose, I just know it. We've been going through this for several months now. She's done it right before so I know she can do it. She just refuses to obey me. If she really respected me, she would obey me.

"You went potty in your pants. I'll just have to spank you."

"No, no, Mommy. I won't do it again." Her pleading seemed to confirm my speculation.

"From now on you're to go in the potty chair. Do you hear?" Hitting her wet bottom and gritting my teeth, I grumbled, "I am sick and tired of wet pants … dirty pants … puddles on the carpet … loads of extra laundry … getting up in the middle of the night to change your soaking sheets."

My tortured thoughts ricocheted in my mind. *You're so much trouble. I can't do anything or go anyplace when I want. You demand love I don't have. Why did I ever want to be a mother.*

My right hand snapped out and slapped across her cheek. Her horrified face stared at me frozen. Suddenly, Darcy gulped in a huge breath and began screaming hysterically. A red mark formed on her cheek. "Oh God, no."

I ran out of the bathroom. Making my way out the door to the back patio, I pounded my fists into my thighs and cursed myself. "How can I do this again? I've been doing so well for a few days. Oh, God, please help me. I'm out of control again."

Maybe I should call someone for help. If I call my pastor, what will his reaction be? I've never had any kind of therapy before. What would people think of me?

I thought of my friends in our women's neighborhood Bible study which I led.

How can I tell them I'm going for counseling? They might not respect me anymore. They might think God doesn't have the answers. After all, if he hasn't helped me, they'll think he can't help them.

"No," I told myself out loud. "I'm just going to have to deal with this myself. I know God can help me. I just haven't found the exact answers yet, but I know I'll do better. Maybe if I increase my devotional time and read more Christian books, it will help. And when Larry becomes the godly man he promised he would be, then

I'll really be able to be godly too."

I could hear Darcy crying in the bathroom. *Oh, thank you, Jesus, Larry is gone. He just doesn't understand how I can get so angry. I try to tell him, but he can't believe it. I suppose I should be grateful he doesn't feel anger like I do, but if he did, at least he could sympathize with my feelings.*

Taking a deep breath, I walked back to the bathroom. When Darcy saw me, she backed up to the wall. "It's okay, Darcy. I'm not mad anymore." I tried to reassure her. But when she didn't relax, my heart only felt heavier. I dried her off and then put another pair of training pants on her. The red mark on her cheek was slowly fading.

"Darcy, please remember. The next time you have to go potty, come into the bathroom and use the potty chair. Mommy has a piece of candy for you if you go potty in the potty chair. Mommy doesn't want to get angry with you, but I really think you're ready to be a big girl and wear big girl panties. Then you won't have to wear baby diapers. You can be a big girl with panties like Mommy wears."

Darcy's tear-stained face looked up at me, attempting to smile. "Okay, Mommy, I try."

The next day before Larry left for a realtors meeting, I asked, "Do you think Darcy's ready to be potty trained?"

"Well, I don't know. How has she been doing?"

"Not very well. At times she manages just fine, but then she'll go for a long time without success. Sometimes I wonder if she wets her pants on purpose."

Larry laughed. "You sound like you think she hates you and wants to get even."

All of a sudden his comment didn't sound so far-fetched. "I wonder if I do."

"Oh, come on, Kathy. She's just a little girl." He stared at me with a confused look.

"No, really. Sometimes when she disobeys me, I think she's doing it on purpose to show me I'm not a good mother. And when she has her temper tantrums, I think I'm a bad mother because I can't make her happy."

"I didn't think you were supposed to make her happy." Larry gathered his papers and stuffed them into his briefcase.

"But what about the joys of motherhood I always hear about? I'm not a very joyful mother these days."

"Well, I know it's not easy to be a mother, but I don't think you're supposed to be joyful all the time. You're not perfect, you know."

"I guess I'm not. I just want to be. If I'm a Christian and God can help me, why aren't I doing better?"

Larry looked wrapped in thought as he paused after picking up the briefcase off the counter.

I felt desperate to continue the conversation. For once we were actually talking without yelling. "What are you thinking?"

He stared at me. "I wonder if you want Darcy to be potty trained as early as possible so she is a credit to your successful mothering?"

"Oh, that's ridiculous …" Then I caught myself. "I really hadn't thought of it that way before. I know I don't want to continually change diapers. But maybe I also want her as a billboard for my mothering accomplishments. Darcy's almost two-and-a half. I thought for sure she would be trained by now. Abby's daughter is. But maybe she's not ready. I think I'll give her a few more days and see what happens."

"That sounds good. But hey, I'm late for the meeting. I have to testify in court after my realtor's meeting so I'll see you after my shift tonight." He gave me a quick peck on the cheek and waved to Darcy. Her face lit up as she continued to dress her doll.

The next few days were disastrous. Instead of getting better, Darcy had more accidents. I wondered if my recent outburst had set her back.

All right, Lord, I think you're showing me she's not ready, so I'll put her back in diapers. I guess it's better than washing a load of training pants every day.

Darcy didn't object to being put back in diapers. I was surprised. In fact, she immediately seemed happier and more obedient. Well, maybe I did the right thing for once in my motherhood career.

CHAPTER 4
NEVER ON TOP

April 1

"Mommy, Mommy, wake up. I hungry."

Roused from my peaceful dream world, I wanted to push away Darcy's insistent plea. *Oh no, not so soon. I was awake nursing Mark only minutes ago. How many times did he wake up last night ... three ... four?* My fogged mind had lost count. I focused my eyes on the digital clock next to the bed and moaned as I read 5:49.

"Darcy, you can play in your room for a while. I'm too tired to get up right now. Let Mommy sleep a little longer."

"No. No. I hungry. Come, Mommy, come." She tugged at the sheets.

Larry murmured in his sleep beside me. I knew no amount of pleading could convince Darcy to leave me alone. Her begging would only wake Larry and he hadn't gotten to sleep until 3:30 because of investigating a car crash.

"Okay, just a second. Let me put on my slippers." Only determination pulled my body out of the warm bed as exhaustion adhesively clung to my muscles.

I stumbled into the kitchen. Dirty dinner dishes lay scattered on the counter, painfully reminding me I had decided not to wash them the night before. *Why had I thought it would be easier to do them this morning?* Then I remembered. I had taken the time to vacuum the carpet instead because it was littered with Darcy's cracker crumbs. I felt better. At least one thing was clean.

I piled greasy dishes into the sink and started cooking oatmeal. I smiled as I remembered my family's reunion would be held in the mountains the next day. Thoughts of sitting outside the rented cabin in the cool, fresh air, and visiting with family inspired me to work even faster.

Then, out of the corner of my eye, I noticed Darcy running through the family room. Her foot caught on the plant stand sending the philodendron to the floor. Darcy lay sprawled and crying on the floor amidst soil, bits of leaves, and broken pottery.

Anger rose within me like hot lava. "My clean carpet! Darcy, look at what you've done now," I yelled.

Gritting my teeth to contain my exploding rage, I grasped Darcy's arms and yanked her to her feet.

Darcy's chin quivered as she attempted to control her sobs. "Hurt, Mommy. Owee."

A voice within said, "It was an accident. She's so little." Suddenly, my heart softened. Unexpectedly, I remembered the last thought I had before I drifted off to sleep the night before, *Lord, I commit tomorrow to you and whatever you might have in store for me.*

"It's all right, Darcy. I know it was an accident," I brushed the dirt off her pajamas.

I looked down at the broken pieces of blue poetry littering the floor and started crying. "That's the planter my neighbors gave me when daddy died. I hope I can glue it together. Lord, it's just not fair. Not only does it seem like I can't go anywhere, I can't even spend my time in a clean house. And everything gets broken. Why did I have kids anyway?"

Vacuuming up the soil, I couldn't control the tears dribbling down my face. *I am so sick and tired of never having this house clean. There is always something needing done. Before Darcy was born I only needed to spend two or three hours a week cleaning and everything would stay nice for days. Now I spend every day cleaning one mess after another and picking up countless toys along the way. Any of the time I dream of setting aside for myself is consumed by endless loads of laundry and stacks of dirty dishes. I can't put my favorite knickknacks on the coffee table and now, even my favorite planter is broken!* My self-pitying monologue continued in my mind until the dirt was gone and breakfast served.

Later that morning, Darcy started sneezing and soon I was wiping her runny nose. By that evening, her stuffy nose and hacking cough confirmed my worst fears: she had a cold.

"Wouldn't you know it? Wouldn't you just know it?" I whined. "We're supposed to leave for the mountains tomorrow and Darcy gets sick. Why can't the Lord have a little mercy on me? I want to go so desperately. If Darcy doesn't get any worse I'm going anyway, no matter what. I just don't care. My fun isn't going to be spoiled by a sick kid."

Larry's frown made me realize I couldn't risk contaminating everyone else including my elderly grandmother. The next day as Darcy's cold worsened, I moaned, "Why is God punishing me? I know I deserve it but I have always believed he is loving and forgiving. I've seen him work in other areas of my life. Why is this problem so different?"

As the day progressed, I unsuccessfully attempted to believe God loved me. *I must not be very lovable if Darcy constantly disobeys and Larry won't fix the leaking bathroom faucet no matter how many times I remind him. Only baby Mark seems a little happy with me. Thank God, he's a contented baby. I hope he doesn't have the terrible twos like Darcy is in. Lord, don't do that to me! I just won't be able to handle it.*

Larry left the house earlier than usual, saying he needed to work on a flight plan. After Darcy and Mark went down for their naps at one o-clock, I tried to straighten up the mess. Eventually I became so weary I lay on my bed, convinced I would rest for just a few minutes. *Just a few minutes, Lord. Please keep the kids asleep.*

My body jerked as I awoke abruptly and glanced at the clock. 3:05. *I can't believe it. Darcy doesn't usually sleep this long. She's not even coughing. Wow, I feel pretty good. But the house ... Now, I've wasted all that time.*

I jumped up and threaded my way through the house straightening the clutter. Each room looked better. I had accomplished something. *I guess a nap is a good idea. I'll have to take more of them.*

But my pleased feelings soon surrendered to self-pity as I thought about the fun everyone—except me—was having at the reunion. Through dinner and into the evening my warring thoughts battled for control of my mind.

The Lord gave me a good afternoon. I got to rest and still picked up the house.

Yeah, but why couldn't I go to the mountains? God could have protected Darcy from getting sick.

He must have wanted me to stay home for some reason.

Yeah, but I could have been a witness for him to my family.

So on and on the warfare continued.

The next few days I noticed when a joyful attitude temporarily won a skirmish, I had more energy. When boredom and selfishness reigned, my energy level decreased and depression raised the victory flag.

Several days later as I listened to a Christian radio station, a pastor shared a message about the importance of memorizing God's Word. Of course I had done that in the past but now I wondered if this could be a part of the solution I needed. Since my devotional book featured Psalm 42, I read with interest verse 11. "Why are you cast down, O my soul, and why are you in turmoil within me? Hope in God; for I shall again praise him, my salvation and my God."

Oh thank you, Lord. This is me right now. I'll memorize this verse and every time I start to feel discouraged or tired I'll say it.

My inner dialogue turned into praise. Each time a debilitating thought entered my mind, I repeated the verse. Soon all I had to think was the word "hope" and a smile came to my face. I took a nap every day. Physically and spiritually stronger, now I handled well Darcy's sickly disposition and Mark's frequent night feedings.

My spirit sang. I was on the way to victory. After all, hadn't I passed the test of coping with Darcy's sickness and my exhaustion? It had been more than a week since I had been out of control. I knew I would never hurt Darcy again.

CHAPTER 5

TRUSTING

April 15

"Larry, Mark has been sneezing all day. Do you think he's coming down with Darcy's cold?"

"Well, I suppose he certainly could be." Larry seemed clueless as to the monumental meaning I was referring to.

"You know what that means, don't you?" I impatiently interjected. "We might not be able to go to your parents' house for Easter. Remember? We're supposed to leave next week."

"Oh, that's right." It was as if a light bulb went on in his brain. Sometimes I wondered if he ever looked at a calendar. He knew the days he should work and that's all he cared about. Then as if the light bulb burned brighter, he said, "And since I'm flying us in the Cessna, we won't have an air-pressurized cabin. That could hurt his ears if he's congested."

I wanted to say, "Duh! Yes, oh, fearless leader." But instead fearful thoughts swirled around in my head. I felt like kicking trust and faith out the door in locked suitcases. *What if we can't go? I'm so looking forward to getting away to Larry's parents' home. Even though it's a little more difficult taking care of the kids there, it's nice to talk to adults and not be responsible for meals and cleaning. I really need some time to relax. Larry and I can play tennis at the local high school or take walks in the clear, crisp, evening desert air.*

"Oh, please, Lord, heal Mark of his cold. I've been good with Darcy and promise to continue. And remember, I didn't get to go to the reunion, so could you please make Mark better by next week?"

Four-month-old Mark continued to sneeze and the next day it was difficult for him to nurse. He couldn't breathe through his stuffy nose. Gently stroking his short blonde hair away from his warm forehead, I whispered, "Father, I'm believing you'll make Mark better soon." I couldn't tell if my heart was appealing or demanding.

But if I believe, then why do these nagging doubts harass me like a pesky fly incessantly circling my head?

"Lord, I'm trying to believe. Help my unbelief."

The next morning, I opened my eyes slowly, surprised the sun was already up and the house was still quiet. Hadn't Darcy woken yet? I guessed not. For just a few moments I relaxed as the sunshine ignored the drapes and craftily invaded the room. Larry slept peacefully beside me. I climbed out of bed, went to the window, and turned on the air conditioner's fan. Its steady, dull buzzing would help drown out the morning commotion so he could sleep.

Walking through the quietness, I breathed a sigh of gratitude. "Thank you, Father. Mark's congestion hasn't prevented him from sleeping."

But then my apprehension of the previous day resurfaced. *What if Mark isn't well enough to go in the plane?*

I began fixing oatmeal knowing Darcy would wake up soon, trying to shove my distrust to a corner of my mind like a child attempting to push down the puppet in a jack-in-the-box.

Only a few minutes later I heard Darcy's bedroom door open. She walked sleepily into the kitchen rubbing your eyes, her favorite faded pink blanket trapped under one arm.

"Hi, Sweetheart. Did you sleep well?"

"Mommy, what we do today?"

"It's Monday so we're going to Bible study. You get to play with the children at Julie's house."

"Goody, goody," she exclaimed as she broke into a little skip.

Hearing the recently learned phrase "goody, goody," made me giggle. Darcy looked so cute as her little round face lit up with excitement. She could be so darling. The ambivalence of my feelings pierced my heart as I realized how much I loved her when she was good and how much I hated her when she disobeyed.

My thoughts were interrupted as the telephone rang. It was Esther, our regular babysitter. She was sick and wouldn't be able to babysit. I thanked her for calling and hung up.

Oh, no, who am I going to get this late? Sometimes I wish I weren't in charge of this study. I quickly finished preparing breakfast. *Please, Lord, help me find someone else. I don't want to have to stay with all the kids. You know how much I look forward to being with the gals.*

The fear of not finding a babysitter and not being able to go to my in-laws' haunted the recesses of my mind as I quickly dressed Darcy and Mark. Darcy jabbered her usual one hundred baby words a minute, but I didn't seem to hear as I mentally made a list of women to call.

"Mommy! Mommy! I want to paint." Darcy's repetitious whine finally permeated my brooding.

"No, Darcy, you can't paint this morning. We don't have time. I still have to get ready for Bible study and find a babysitter."

"No, Mommy. I want to paint."

Darcy's insistence graded on my nerves as if someone were scratching their fingernails on a blackboard.

"Darcy," I shouted, "I said no. Now stop your whining." I cringed inside knowing my tone was as whiny as hers.

My jumbled thoughts tumbled over themselves. *Mark's not getting better. I've got to get a babysitter. I don't want to stay with the children.*

Darcy's face turned red. She started screaming, jumping up and down in rage. I grabbed her arm, whirled her around, and smacked her on the behind ... hard ... four, then five times. "You stop that right now."

As I yanked her into the air by one arm, I heard a crack from her shoulder. Yet I still carried her, feet dangling in the air, into her bedroom and pushed her onto the floor. "Now stay there until you can be quiet."

After slamming the bedroom door behind me, I stood trembling in the hall listening carefully, fearfully expecting Larry to emerge from our bedroom. But I only heard the noisy window air conditioner.

I walked to the phone. *I've got enough to think about without putting up with her nonsense.* I started calling my list of babysitters but exhausted it with no one available. Tears blurred my vision. *I don't want to spend two-and-a-half hours with the children. I can't even handle my own. It's almost 9:00, only thirty more minutes. I guess I don't have any choice now.* I dressed quickly and ran a comb through my hair.

I called Sally who co-led with me. Thankfully, it was her turn to lead. "Esther is sick. I can't find anyone to babysit. I'll take care of the kids."

"Kathy, just a minute. My mother is here visiting. I'll ask her to take care of them. She loves children."

"Do you think she would?" The hope in my voice made me feel guilty so I quickly added, "No, I couldn't ask her to do that. It wouldn't be fair."

"Oh, it's OK. Hold on, let me go ask her."

My heart beat hard. "Oh, Lord, please make her want to do it. Please!"

Sally came back on the phone. "Kathy, she says she'll be glad to. Really, she loves to do things like this. I'll be leading this week so she doesn't have anything to do anyway."

I couldn't hide my enthusiasm. "Oh, that's great. I'm so glad. I'll meet you at Julie's house."

"Thank you, Lord, you did it. I still can't believe it. Thank you, thank you!" I felt like falling to my knees in thanksgiving but I had to get the kids ready.

I rushed to Darcy's room. Darcy, surrounded by her dolls and stuffed animals, looked up at me.

"We go now, Mommy?"

"Yes, honey, we're going. I'm sorry I got angry with you earlier. But we have to hurry now." I knelt beside her, pressing gently on her shoulder.

"Does that hurt?"

"No."

I breathed a sigh of relief when I couldn't feel anything wrong. I quickly dressed her. As we walked to Julie's house, Darcy grabbed my hand and skipped along beside me as I carried Mark. She looked so happy. I felt so horrible. *Darcy, I'm sorry. I'm trying. I'm really trying. If I ever injure you, I'll kill myself. I couldn't stand it.* Tears flowed down my face. *Oh, Lord, I'm still getting angry. Please help me.*

A few minutes later at Bible study, as the six of us sat around Sally's dining room table studying Ephesians, I continued to thank the Lord I was there. When it was time for prayer requests, I asked they pray for Mark to recover quickly from his cold. As one of the ladies prayed for him, I felt hopeful, yet doubt still surged in the back of my mind.

The next day Mark seemed worse and my faith plummeted like a glider caught in a down-draft.

That week I struggled to build a wall of faith, but continually allowed examples of God's negative responses to my prayers interfere with my construction. Then I recalled how God had supplied a babysitter for the children and another small wall was erected. Back and forth, the bricks were piled high and then knocked down again. Forgetting to use the mortar of Scripture truths, I appeared to be a clumsy stonemason.

On Friday, Mark seemed slightly better. He took a long nap and nursed better than he had all week. My hopes soared. I planned what I would pack for the trip.

Saturday morning arrived and the moment of decision faced us. Larry and I talked it over and finally decided the remaining congestion was not serious enough to cause Mark's ears to hurt while in the plane.

As we flew out of the airport Sunday morning, I cautiously nursed Mark to keep him sucking so his ears would stay clear. During our flight, I reflected on the past week and berated myself for my fluctuating faith. *Lord, all my worrying didn't do a single bit of good. Why couldn't I have just trusted you all along? It was your grace in answer to all the prayers making Mark better for this trip. Worrying only made me tense and unhappy and didn't change a thing. I blew it again, didn't I? I lost control with Darcy for the zillionth time. When am I ever going to master my anger?*

I looked at sleeping Darcy in the back seat. The softened features of her face made her look angelic and peaceful as if she could never do anything wrong. *Darcy, I'm sorry. I'm trying. I'm really trying. How will you ever grow up to be a normal human being with how I've treated you? And for sure you'll never love me. I've hurt you so horribly.*

Tears flowed down my face. I looked out the side window so Larry wouldn't see my grief. The houses and cars below looked small and unimportant. *Lord, is my anger ever going to be an insignificant part of my life? Will I ever be able to look back and see how you helped me control it?*

I was afraid to think any further. *I must live one day at a time. Today is Easter Sunday, the day Jesus rose from the dead. I'm going to believe I have resurrected control over my anger and my doubts starting with this trip. Thank you, Father, we're going. I know it's a gift from you.*

CHAPTER 6

BITTERSWEET

April 30

As I finished dusting the living room furniture, I turned to Larry. "Honey, have you noticed the bills stacking up since we got home from visiting your parents? When do you think you'll be able to send them off?" I tried not to sound as uptight as I felt.

"Oh, I guess I can do them before I go to work. But I want to finish this article first."

For a moment, I studied Larry relaxing in the blue corduroy lounge chair and reading the magazine that seemingly represented the barrier between us.

"Honey, it wouldn't take more than fifteen minutes to write out those checks. Could you take care of it now, please?" I tried to sound as patient as I wanted to feel, but I knew the edge in my tone betrayed me.

Glancing up at me, he tartly replied, "Kathy, don't worry about it. I'll do it later."

Don't worry about it? Doesn't he know how much I hate to see bills accumulate? But I caught myself. *I'm not going to nag him. I must trust the Lord. It's not my responsibility anymore. Now he will have to deal with the consequences if the bills aren't paid. But Father, please motivate him. Don't you think as Christians we should pay our bills on time?*

But then the thought of late charges, when we barely had enough money to cover the bills, began to gnaw at my determination to trust God. I remembered how I used to agonize over paying the bills on time and how I begged Larry to take over the job. When he had finally said he would, I was glad and so relieved. Now I wondered if I had done the right thing.

As that Monday afternoon passed, I realized it would soon be time for Larry to leave for work and he still hadn't made any move toward the desk. I tried to keep busy putting the kids down for their naps and cleaning up the lunch dishes, but my mind obsessed about overdue bills.

After Larry left for work and I knew he hadn't touched the checkbook, I fled to the family room. *I'm going to scream, God. I can't handle it. If I write out those bills myself, I'll be doing them for the rest of our marriage. I'm not going to do it. He'll just have to pay the consequences. But if he would just cooperate with things like this, I just know I could be more patient and content.* I frantically eyed the room. *What can I do to take my mind off of this?*

I rushed over to the television and jerked it on. I flipped the selector around several times and finally found a soap opera I hadn't watched for several months. I tried to reassure myself, "Now, I'm not going to get hooked again. I'll only watch it today. I've got to do something to get my mind off those bills."

Within the first fifteen minutes, I became reacquainted with the plot. Then a commercial came on advertising a new cake mix. I nestled among the pillows on the couch, enjoying the image of the richly frosted devil's food cake.

"That sure makes my mouth water," I mumbled to myself. I tried to think of any sweets to satisfy my cravings. I smiled as I remembered the large package of candy I had bought. Rustling through the cupboard, I found it and returned to my chair just in time to find out Sue was on trial for murdering her husband even though Kevin had shot him.

By the end of the program, I had finished half the bag of candy. Scouting the kitchen, I finally decided to hide it in the potato bin. I knew Larry wouldn't look there.

The next morning Candace phoned. She wanted me to help her start and teach a ladies' Bible study in her neighborhood.

"Wow, Candy, that's great," I exclaimed. "What a wonderful opportunity. How many are interested in coming?"

She explained her plan for the study and then mentioned, "We're going to have it in the afternoon. That's the best time for this group of women to meet."

"Oh …" I quietly replied, my shoulders drooping with disappointment.

"What wrong, Kathy?"

"That just wouldn't work out for me. My kids take their naps then, and there's no way they can miss them. I guess I won't be able to help you."

After I hung up, the sadness in my heart overwhelmed me. "Lord, I want to serve you so badly. I long to reach out and minister to others. Why won't you let me? Why am I stuck home with these children?"

Glancing over at Darcy as she watched "Sesame Street," I could barely keep from darting hateful glances at her. I knew God wanted me to be a loving mother and raise godly children, but somehow it just didn't satisfy me. I remembered the excitement of starting my own neighborhood Bible study so many years earlier—even before Darcy was born. So many fabulous things had happened as a result. I wanted to reach out to others again—even more than the current study.

Lord, I want to be used by you like that again. Didn't I write down as one of my goals for this year, "start another Bible study?" Instead of evangelizing the world, all I do is pick up toys, change diapers, and wipe runny noses.

For the rest of the day, I thought about the candy waiting in the potato bin and tried to determine whether or not Pamela would tell Mark she was carrying Louis' child.

At three o'clock, I grabbed the candy bag and flicked on the television. A load of guilt lay heavy on my heart. "Well, I don't have anything exciting to do around here, so I might as well see what's happening with them."

The next two weeks were consumed with more and more TV watching and candy eating. The candy filled me up and eventually I only snacked at dinnertime. I was engrossed with the soap opera characters. At times they seemed more real and important than my own family.

By Friday, my patience level had crumbled. I took the children for our usual early evening walk. When Darcy wouldn't stay out of the street, I grabbed her shoulders and shook her violently. Embarrassed by my behavior, I yanked her into one arm, pushed Mark in the stroller with the other, and practically ran home.

"Darcy, if you can't obey me, then we won't go for any more walks. One of these days you'll learn to obey me." Feeling my face flush, I slammed the front door behind us.

Darcy screamed, "Walk. Walk. I want a walk."

Suddenly, I realized how tired I was. My muscles felt as if they were attached to one hundred pound weights. I gazed at the family room. Coloring books, crayons, and bits of crackers littered the floor. I wondered how long it had been since I dusted the furniture. I couldn't remember.

"Now, Kathy, you are really tired, just hang on." I tried to give myself a pep talk. "In just a few hours both kids will be asleep and you'll be able to go to bed too." The thought of the cozy, warm bed made me feel even more exhausted.

The evening dragged. Darcy continued to be keyed up and unhappy. Mark cried for seemingly no reason. I decided he must be teething again. *Does it ever stop?*

Finally, after putting them to bed, I slipped between the sheets of my own bed. *This feels so good. I'm so tired. I hope I'm not getting sick.* "Father, why does it seem like I never get anything done around here? My house is always a mess, I know I'm not a very good mother, and I'm too weary to be a good wife. Am I really worth anything? How can you love me?"

My tired body and heavy heart sucked me into a pit of hopelessness. It seemed as if I would never learn whatever lesson God was trying to teach me. The days merely passed by uneventfully except for the anger wrapping it's strangling cord around my existence.

Maybe I just need a good night's sleep. Help me tomorrow, Father ... But before the thought finished I drifted into a restless sleep, dreaming about Sue being convicted and sent to prison as Kevin laughed diabolically in the background.

CHAPTER 7

FIVE GALLONS

May 10

Mark's hungry cries startled me out of a deep sleep. The sun's rays barely permeated the overcast sky. The high clouds made it seem more like a June morning than one in the middle of May. Dragging myself out of bed, I wondered why I was still so weary. Even after ten hours of sleep, my body felt as though I had just run a marathon.

Plodding through the morning routine, I suspected I was coming down with a cold, but I didn't feel congested. I comforted myself with the promise of a nap.

Mark went down for his nap easily, but Darcy wouldn't settle down. As I lay down on my bed and started to relax, Darcy wandered into my room, her thin, blonde hair damply matted against her head.

"Darcy, you're supposed to be in bed sleeping. Now go back to your room."

"Mommy, me not tired. Can I color, please?" Her bright, alert eyes convinced me she really wasn't sleepy.

"Oh, all right. You can color here on the floor while I rest." A warning bell in my brain signaled potential danger, but I assured myself I would keep an eye on her while I rested.

I got up, found the crayons and coloring book, and spread them out on the carpet beside my bed. "Now remember, Darcy, you color only on the paper and nothing else, okay?"

Her happy face anticipated coloring in her new Lassie coloring book. I smiled, lay back down on the bed, and watched her scribble on the first page.

Oh, this feels so good. My muscles relaxed, and as I closed my eyes, I felt peaceful, more peaceful than I'd felt the last couple of weeks. *This feels too good to be true ...*

Suddenly, I sat up straight. I was still in a daze when I realized I had drifted off to sleep and completely lost track of time--and Darcy. *Oh no, Darcy is gone.* I looked around the room. Half the crayons were scattered about the floor. The closet door featured an assortment of red crayon circles.

"Darcy! Darcy! Where are you?"

Oh, no! All the walls will be crayoned. As I felt a burning flash of anger sear through my body, I wondered whether I was more angry with her or myself.

I ran down the hall, following the crayon-marked walls. Turning the corner to her room, I stared in disbelief as Darcy sat on her bed drawing on the wallpaper.

"Darcy! Look what you've done. You brat, look what you've done! How am I ever going to get all these marks off so Daddy won't know what happened?"

I grabbed Darcy at the shoulders and lifted her into the air. Face to face, I screamed, "Darcy, I told you not to color on the walls. Why won't you behave? Can't you do anything right?"

I shook her. Her head wobbled back and forth as she looked at me in wide-eyed horror. "Brat! Brat! Brat! Sometimes I hate you."

In my mind's eye, I imagined hurling her onto the floor, her body landing with a dull thud. *I'm going to do it. I want to hurt her.*

A second later, the reality of my thought gripped me. I laid her on the bed. "Oh, God!" I sobbed. "I really could have hurt her seriously. I don't hate her. I hate myself. What am I going to do?"

I threw my arms around whimpering Darcy's trembling body and hugged her tight. "I'm sorry. I'm sorry. It was my fault you colored on the walls." I coaxed her into my lap and gently rocked back and forth.

"Why am I so irritable and angry, Darcy? I just don't understand it."

As Darcy cried softly, I surveyed all the bad times we had had during the last couple of weeks and one common denominator stood out: the candy! All that candy was making me tired and irritable. My body was reacting to the sugar. And I hadn't been eating nutritious meals.

"Father, thank you. Thank you for showing me. All right, I won't have any more. I promise."

At three o-clock though, I was haunted by the two candy bars hidden from Larry in the cupboard. I turned on the TV hoping to be diverted.

Trying to concentrate on the program, I eventually glanced into the living room where Darcy played near a five gallon glass bottle of drinking water which the water man had delivered that morning. *I wonder if she could break that bottle? No, I don't think so, it's awfully heavy. How could she possibly push over such a ...* But before I finished my thought, Darcy pushed on the bottle. With a soft crunching sound, the bottle tipped over and broke, spilling five gallons of water onto the green, sculptured carpet. Shocked by the accident, Darcy jumped back, then stared at me in fear.

An overwhelming sensation of surrender flowed through my body as I helplessly watched the water soak into the carpet.

"Yes, I see it, Darcy. It's okay, honey. I'm not going to get angry with you. Mommy wasn't taking good care of you. I finally see how wrong I am."

I turned off the television and began picking up the hundreds of shards of glass.

"Father, you sure got my attention. I confess I've been neglecting my family and I've been eating a lot of junk. I ask you to forgive me."

During the next hour, as I used almost every towel in the house to soak up the water, a thought rumbling through my mind for the last couple of months surfaced again. *I wonder if my children will grow up and say, "My mother didn't have time for me."*

I murmured, "Lord, I don't want my children to say that. I really want them to feel like I'm always available and they are very important to me. I know I complain a lot about being a mother, but actually I want to be a good mother. And I always have wanted to be a mother. I don't know why I have such a hard time enjoying what I really want to be. Why do I, Lord?"

Even though no voice answered, I felt peaceful. Sugar and incessant TV watching were no longer going to dominate me and make me irritable. I was determined to spend my time and energy focusing on the Lord. I knew it was going to be different from now on.

Darcy intently watched me spread towels repeatedly on the carpet and walk on them to help soak up the water. As she joined in, I said, "Darcy, I promise you I'm going to try to spend more time playing with you. Would you like that?"

She ran off and returned carrying her Candyland game. "Can we play now, Mommy?" she pleaded with a huge smile.

I laughed, enjoying her enthusiasm and sparkle. "Oh, my daughter Darcy, you are a live one. As soon as I finish this, we will play Candyland."

CHAPTER 8
BIG DIFFERENCE

May 20

"Darcy, I really need to clean the bathroom right now. Mommy is having a Tupperware party tonight, and I have to clean the house. I know I promised last week to play with you more often, but today I must concentrate on the house."

Darcy's pout wrenched my heart. Even though I had meant what I said the previous week, each day's busy schedule pushed aside my good intentions.

"Okay, how about after I finish the bathrooms? I'll stop for a few minutes and we'll play one game of Candyland."

"Okay, Mommy. I get it ready." Her disappointed pout instantly turned into a radiantly happy smile as she skipped off to her room.

By the time I put out fresh towels, I realized how fast the morning was vanishing. I knew I should bake the cake so it would have time to cool before I frosted it. I wondered if I could start it before playing with Darcy.

It is such a simple game. Why do I dread playing it? I knew why. It seemed like every time we almost reached the winning candy house and the end of the game, one of us would draw the lollipop card or the gumdrop card and would be sent back almost to the beginning. Sometimes the game would continue seemingly forever. And since Darcy inevitably folded the cards or threw them around the room also irritated me. I would be glad when she was older and we could play more sophisticated games.

But if I don't want to play with her now, she probably won't want to play with me then. I feared the consequences of not spending enough time with Darcy in these early years and felt guilty about my selfishness. *Oh, Father, will I ever be the mother I want to be?*

"Well, enough of this," I scolded myself. "I've got to get working."

I tiptoed near the door of Darcy's bedroom and peeked around the corner. She was carefully laying out the colored cards around the Candyland board.

Oh, good. She's busy so I'll go start the cake.

But I had not even finished combining the ingredients when Darcy ran into the kitchen carrying a handful of Candyland cards. "Mommy, play now?" she asked.

"Oh, honey, I'm sorry. I decided to mix this cake first. Can you wait a few more minutes, then we'll play?" I tried to sound cheerful, hoping to ward off a temper tantrum. At first, as her lower lip started to quiver it seemed I was going to be unsuccessful. But then the phone rang.

"Me get it, me get it," she yelled.

"No, Darcy, only Mommy and Daddy answer the phone."

I watched Darcy out of the corner of my eye as she wandered off with drooping shoulders, folding several of the cards in half. *Oh well, at least she didn't have a fit.*

I picked up the receiver and sadly listened as a friend told me she wouldn't be able to come to the Tupperware party. I felt disappointed but tried to sound understanding as I accepted her apology.

Turning my attention back to the cake, I realized I couldn't hear Darcy. I walked into the living room to check on her and stopped short. She was sitting on the fireplace hearth, sprinkled from head to toe with sand from under the gas logs. A thick layer of the sand encircled her on the bricks and carpet.

"Darcy!" I screamed. "What are you doing? I've told you over and over again to stay out of the fireplace. Just look what you've done. I'm trying to keep everything clean for company tonight."

I marched over to her and yanked her to her feet. I spanked her and, even though my hand stung, I continued to hit her again and again. "Damn you! Why can't you do anything right?"

Darcy's screaming egged me on. "Maybe if it hurts enough, you'll obey me next time."

When I could no longer stand the pain in my hand, I pushed Darcy down on the couch. Ignoring her sobs, I jerked the vacuum out of the hall closet, snapped it on, and furiously pushed it back and forth over the sand. Occasionally I glared at her and lectured, "Why do you continue to do the things you know make me so mad? I can't understand it. You'd think my anger would motivate you to obey."

Darcy's tear-filled eyes pleaded with me. When my anger subsided and all the sand had been vacuumed up, I sat down beside her. "Darcy, Mommy has told you before you are not to play in the fireplace. I just don't understand why you keep doing it. I don't want to get angry with you, but I'm so uptight about getting everything done. Please help Mommy by doing what I tell you, all right?"

Darcy rubbed her eyes. I knew I should give her some attention but the thought of not being ready for the party made my neck muscles tighten. "I'll get everything ready for tonight, then I'll have time to play with you," I called out after her.

For the rest of the day, I cleaned the house and prepared the refreshments. Mark woke up early from his nap, was fussy from teething, and needed to be held, so I didn't get everything done as quickly as I'd hoped. It was five o'clock when I finally finished. With a sigh of relief, I plopped Darcy on the floor in front of the television to watch a cartoon while I fixed dinner.

When only eight women arrived for the Tupperware party, I realized there had been no reason to get uptight or angry. They hadn't even used the bathroom which I had cleaned so meticulously. "I should have spent more time playing with Darcy. She's more important."

During the following week, Darcy's behavior continued to deteriorate. Every time I started a cleaning project or sat down to nurse Mark, she found a way to get into trouble. She emptied soil out of the houseplant pots even though I repeatedly spanked her. Her jealousy toward Mark increased. When she thought I wasn't watching, she pinched him or hit him. Her disobedience was getting worse but it seemed as though I was powerless to stop it. Spankings didn't deter her. I thought she would want to avoid my anger but instead, the struggle for power intensified—and so did my guilt and my blame of Larry.

If only he were here to help me, I wouldn't be like this. I need his help. Aren't we supposed to be parents together? Suddenly, a memory surfaced unbidden; something I hadn't dwelt upon for a long time. When Larry and I were dating, he remarked, "I don't want to have kids. I'd rather do other things."

I was totally taken off guard by his comment. It was inconceivable to me. Not have children? "But Larry, I've wanted children all my life. I've always wanted to be a mom. We're engaged. How will that work?"

"Well, I guess you'll just have to take care of them. I've been an only child my whole life and never ever wanted to have a brother or sister. I've been just fine without other kids around. I don't even have cousins I'm close to. They live in other states and we rarely see them, maybe once a year, and aren't in contact. You know all this, Kathy. You know how my family is. I'm just fine without having children. It's just not important to me at all."

I couldn't remember exactly what happened then but I did remember my absolute shock at such a conversation. *No one doesn't want children. A family is just too important. Larry knew I lived a block from my cousins and the Collard brothers did everything together.* My mom's parents had died by the time she was ten and she raised us teaching family was too important and we should make every member a priority. She didn't have anyone and she was determined we knew who family was. She had even told me one of the contributing reasons she married my dad was because of his family who lived next door. Mrs. Collard, my grandmother, welcomed her into their home as the little girl who needed love and attention. She was lonely, being raised by a maiden aunt who worked full time. An older brother lived in the house but he treated my mom badly. She longed for him to treat her better. All our family knew the stories and family meant everything.

Not have children? I didn't know what to say so I said nothing. "He'll change his mind after we're married. There's just no way he can keep this insane idea. He'll see the truth soon."

Now Larry and I had been married for seven years and he lived out that insane idea every day, making his other priorities superior. Working on the street as a cop was thrilling for him. "I'd do this for free," he enthusiastically told others. He often described all the money he would make with the big commercial real estate opportunities he had going, but nothing ever panned out. Being a cop and flying were his loves. And I wondered if he had a mistress on the side. It would make perfect sense. He wasn't interested in me. I felt paralyzed knowing how to figure it all out and how to change him.

Oh sure, he paid some attention to Darcy and Mark, but it wasn't wholehearted. Sometimes my heart broke when I saw his cursory responses. At least he was willing to have his hard-earned money spent to care for them. He was an honorable man. *It's not enough. Maybe I shouldn't have married him after all. He gave me the warning. I just couldn't imagine it could be true. If only I had a job, it would be easy to divorce him. Then I could provide for me and the children.*

The very idea terrified me. Plus, shouldn't a Christian not divorce? My emotions dragged from one confusing thought to another.

But regardless of what degree Larry deserved blame, I still had to face I was responsible for my own actions. It was becoming obvious my anger was largely at the root of Darcy's temper tantrums, with help from her daddy paying little attention to her. I kept thinking if I wouldn't get so angry with her, she wouldn't disobey. If Larry gave her much more attention, she wouldn't disobey either. The more I thought about it, the more I realized I was trying to be perfect. For some reason, I believed if I were perfect, Darcy would be too. *That's ridiculous. You'll never be perfect and neither will Darcy.* I knew then I should work on getting my anger in control but not expect Darcy to always obey me. After all, what child did? Somehow, the realization relieved my mind and help me see other truths.

I did need to give Darcy more attention. I was neglecting to fill her emotional needs. "Oh, Lord, is there no hope? I want to be a perfect mother but I'm so horrible. Why does cleaning the house seem more important than giving her attention?"

As I surveyed the house, I realized a neat house gave me tangible proof I had accomplished something. When I gave Darcy attention, I didn't have any concrete evidence I had done anything worthwhile. She still disobeyed me. Plus, I didn't feel very loved myself. I had nothing to give, it seemed.

I longed for the days before Darcy was born when Larry and I did so much together. Larry had been the companion and best friend I'd always wanted. But now our lives were so busy, we were growing farther apart My nagging and negative desperate pleas for Larry's attention only widened the gap between us.

Just as I begged for Larry's attention, Darcy's disobedience pleaded with me, "I need you. I want your attention and approval." I couldn't admit God had built into Darcy and Mark that longing for attention for which I was supposed to represent God. And later, they would transfer that need to him.

To acknowledge that would spell feeling even more like a failure. More things I didn't do right. I could only think of my needs and would respond harshly to Darcy: "Then why don't you obey me and be a good girl?" Little did I know her answer would have been: "Because then you won't pay attention to me at all."

Several weeks later at Bible study, one of the women raved about a book on disciplining children she had read and I borrowed it. It talked about the importance of consistently giving consequences. I recognized sometimes I reacted patiently and gave Darcy a consequence but other times I ignored her disobedience or got furious, spanking her out of control. For the first time I also realized my anger was not going to force an obedient spirit in her.

"Oh, Lord, please help me to be consistent."

I was excited. I couldn't wait for Darcy to misbehave so I could try the next disciplinary techniques I had learned. I didn't have to wait long.

The next morning I discovered Darcy playing with the telephone. Just two days before, I had yelled and spanked her for doing the very same thing and here she was, doing it again. Anger started to well up inside me. "Okay, Father, give me self-control and empower me to give a consequence without anger."

I took a deep breath and and walked over to her. "Darcy, you know you are not supposed to play with the telephone." Then I almost said, "I'm going to spank you because you played with the telephone," but I remembered the phrase the book had suggested and I had memorized. I said, "Darcy, I'm going to spank you so you'll remember not to play with the telephone the next time."

I gently guided her to her bedroom and told her to stay there. I went to the kitchen and took the wooden spoon out of the drawer. As I walked from the kitchen to her bedroom, I reminded myself I was training Darcy, not taking revenge for her disobedience. I was surprised at how calm I remained.

When I returned to Darcy's room she mischievously grinned at me, probably reasoning she wasn't in trouble because I wasn't angry. Picking her up and holding her close, I explained again. "Mommy is spanking you because I love you and because I want you to remember not to play with the telephone." I gave her three quick swats across the bottom. She started crying as if she were going to have a temper tantrum, but I continued to hold her close. She stopped crying within two minutes. Blinking back tears, she penitently murmured, "No more telephone, Mommy."

I wanted to jump for joy. "Oh, thank you, Jesus, this is the way it's supposed to be. I didn't get angry. I didn't spank her too hard."

For the next couple of days I calmly used the spoon each time Darcy disobeyed. Soon, all I had to do was tell her I was going to get the spoon and she would immediately obey.

After another successful time of disciplining her correctly with a consequence, a thought suddenly popped into my mind and I grabbed a piece of paper. I drew a line down the middle and on the left side labeled "misbehavior." On the other side, I wrote, "consequence." After filling it out with several ideas, I taped it to the refrigerator. Now I had some concrete way to remind myself of what to do, rather than being so uncertain and confused.

"I'm actually doing something right, God. Thank you for leading me. Please help this to make a difference."

CHAPTER 9

CAN'T SAY NO

May 30

"Hi, is Kathy Miller home, please?"

I shifted the telephone receiver to the other ear. "Yes, this is she."

"Hi, Kathy, I'm Ruth from the church office. We're calling to see whether you'd consider teaching one of the preschool Sunday school classes this summer. Our summer session starts in two weeks on June 13th, and lasts until school starts. We'd really love to have you help us and the children."

Hesitating, I grappled for words. "Well, uh ... Oh, I see. Well ... I have taught a children's Sunday school class before but that was a long time ago."

"I can understand your concern, but our teaching materials are excellent, and of course, you'd have an assistant to help you."

My thoughts tumbled over each other. *I wonder whether she would be so quick to ask me if she knew I was a child abuser. Considering I can barely cope with my own kids, I wonder how I'd handle the pressure of teaching. But they always need people to help. I really should do my part.*

The gaping pause was awkward. I strained to find something to say. "Well, I'd like to help because I really appreciate everything my daughter learns in Sunday school. Uh, I guess there's no reason why I can't …" I caught myself. *Lord, give me courage right now.* "… but I really should talk it over with my husband. How about if I call you back tomorrow?"

"That would be fine. I'll look forward to hearing from you. Bye."

I hung up and anxiously faced the reality of knowing what Larry would say. He usually contended I had too much to do already and should drop some of my activities. I would defend my position and say I needed opportunities to get out of the house. I certainly wasn't looking forward to talking with him about this.

As I thought more about teaching the class, I began to wrestle with my feelings of "duty." *Kathy, shouldn't you do your part? If Darcy's receiving, you should be giving. If you don't do it, who will?*

Visualizing Darcy's faithful teacher and her happy, welcoming smile each Sunday, I wondered if I could find joy in taking care of other children when I didn't enjoy my own.

Late the next morning after Larry woke up, I explained, "Larry, one of the ladies from church called yesterday and asked me to teach a children's Sunday school class for the summer months. You know, Darcy learns so much at church, and I want to do my part. What do you think about it? I bet I could handle it. I'm sure it wouldn't take very much time." I hesitantly smiled at him, trying to appear convinced myself.

His eyebrows frowned over his hazel eyes. "Well, I'm not so sure you have the time to do it. And even if the preparation time were small, you'd still have to meet a deadline. That's added pressure. Right now you barely have enough energy to keep the house clean."

I could feel a mass of hurt begin to grow within me. "But, Larry, I really feel obligated to help. What if no one helped? Darcy wouldn't be learning more about Jesus."

Larry's grin assured me he knew I wasn't really convinced myself. "Honey, you just don't have enough time or energy. You are so busy with Mark--he's just a baby. And Darcy is a handful. I'm proud of you for wanting to help, but you'll just have to trust the Lord to supply someone else to fill the gap. He can do it, you know."

When Larry rose from his chair, I knew the discussion was over. I reluctantly admitted to myself what he said was true, but guilt overwhelmed me anyway. *Why do I have such a hard time saying no to anyone? That must be the hardest thing for me to do. I've accepted more commitments than I can handle just because I couldn't refuse someone's request.*

For most of the day, I tried to get up the nerve to call Ruth back. Over and over, I rehearsed my lame-sounding excuses. By the end of the day, I still hadn't called. Every time the phone rang, I jumped fearing it might be her.

Shortly after dinner, I discovered Darcy playing with the telephone for the second time that day. "Darcy, how many times have I told you you can't play with the telephone? Why do you keep doing it?"

Then it hit me. I had been so uptight about calling Ruth I hadn't been disciplining Darcy or giving her attention. I'd been giving her all sorts of yelled warnings but no action—good or bad.

I smiled at her. "Well, little girl, I guess it's time to get back on course again."

The next morning I forced myself to dial the church's number. When Ruth answered, I explained my husband didn't think I had enough time to fulfill such a responsibility. I falteringly went on to explain our son was still a baby and required a lot of attention.

As I went on and on with all my excuses, I knew I was verbalizing insecurity.

Ruth politely accepted my explanation and said she was sure the Lord would provide someone to teach. I hoped so, but wondered how he could if people like me didn't do their part.

Feeling foolish, I hung up. *Your immaturity shows when you can't give a simple explanation. What a weak faith you have when you can't trust the Lord to fulfill a need.*

Larry had been down the hall and walked into the kitchen. "Honey, I heard your call. Why can't you just say you can't do it? Why do you have to give so many excuses? I don't have any trouble just saying no. You can too."

I looked at him and wanted to yell, *Just because it's easy for you, Larry, doesn't mean I can too. You think you're so perfect, of course you think you have the right way.* But knowing he was right, and since I'd been asking myself the same question, my anger dissipated. "I don't know. I just know when I was a little girl every report card said I was conscientious and dependable. Those labels made me feel so important and like a good girl. I always said yes to everything my teacher told me to do. Maybe saying no seems like the opposite and then I'll feel bad about myself? I don't know."

Larry looked thoughtful. "Hmmm. Sounds like it makes sense. Maybe by looking at yourself through God's eyes that he sees you good not because of all you do but because of your being his forgiven daughter could help. That's something secure, not whether or not you say yes or no."

I hated to admit it, but I replied, "That's interesting. I will think more about that."

Even as I signed in relief, guilt knocked again at the back door of my emotions. But I didn't let him in. "No. No! I'm not going to feel guilty again. I've got too much to do now without taking on new responsibilities. I've got to work on controlling my anger," I cried out, trying to convince myself.

The more I thought of our conversation, the more the ideas began to make sense. I was always trying to look good in people's eyes rather than believing God's view of me. I was shocked that Sunday when our pastor's sermon was entitled, "Who You Are In Christ." What? Did someone tell him I needed this? He talked about how we are clothed in Jesus' righteousness and nothing can destroy or distract from his seeing his saved children in that way.

The Lord seemed to be weaving threads of understanding, even healing, because I also remembered something a friend had shared with me several months earlier. Wanda explained, "Y'know, Kathy, what has been helping me about time commitments? 'An opportunity is not necessarily God's open door.' I heard it at a conference."

I must have looked confused because she explained, "If someone expresses an opportunity, it doesn't necessarily mean God intends me to accept the responsibility or accept the challenge."

My heart felt lighter. "Okay, I'm not going to feel guilty for what God doesn't want me to do. Teaching a class is an opportunity but God hasn't called me to it."

As the day went along and I thought of the phrase again and again, I realized if I accepted a project or responsibility God didn't want me to take on, I would be taking away an opportunity from the person who God truly intended for it. I would be robbing her of being blessed because he wants her to give of herself and receive from others. And if I take on something not his will, I won't have the time and energy to take on what he really wants me to do.

This was starting to take shape in my mind. *I don't have to feel guilty. It's up to God to supply for every need; not me. I'm only supposed to do what he wants me to do. I can say no if that's his will.*

I chuckled to myself as I thought of how often Larry teased me by saying, "Assert yourself!" Now, I knew how I would reply the next time: "No!"

CHAPTER 10

SUICIDE

June 8

"Larry, have you thought any more about going to the church picnic tomorrow? I really want you to go. It'll be such a great opportunity for us to have a family outing and Darcy is looking forward to it."

Even as I spoke, my soul beseeched, *Please give him a desire to go, Lord.* When I had first mentioned it to him earlier in the week, he hadn't been sure he'd go. So I had prayed all week he would change his mind.

Larry turned away. "Well, it looks like I'm going to have a real estate appointment tomorrow."

"If it's in the morning you could come after you finish."

Dropping onto the couch, Larry riveted his eyes on me. "Kathy, I don't want to go, okay? I'm sorry, but it just doesn't sound like something I'd enjoy. You know how people respond to me after hearing I'm a cop. They just complain about their tickets or something wrong other cops have done to them. I don't need that. I get enough of it on the street. You go and have a good time with the kids."

A lump grew in my throat and tears darted into my eyes as my spirits plummeted to the ground.

"Honey, I just don't understand why you don't want to go with us. Please come. Please!"

"Kathy, this isn't the only activity for families, you know." *Is that a sneer in his voice?* "We'll do something together another time."

I turned and walked out of the room, tears streaming down my face. *Lord, am I so wrong to want us to do things together? Are his real estate deals and avoiding hearing complaints more important than his family? He should just get over it.*

I wanted to bang my fists against heaven's gates, demanding an answer. *Father, why don't you change Larry? Why don't you make him want to spend more time with us? I'm so lonely. It's his fault I'm so angry. If you change him, I can be the contented, patient woman you want me to be.*

Larry followed me into the bedroom. I brushed away my tears before he could see them.

"Kathy, are you upset? I promise we'll do something another time."

I wanted to fling abuse at him, to pour out my hurt and let it sting him too, but what good would it do? I knew it would only create an unresolved argument.

I began making the bed and in contrived cheerfulness replied, "As much as I want you to go, I can't force you if you think you won't have a good time."

"Thank you." His smile deepened my pain.

"Oh, by the way. I've left my off-duty pistol here in the dresser drawer since I'll be going on a real estate appointment. It's in the top drawer so it's high enough Darcy can't reach it but I wanted you to know."

I mumbled, "Okay."

The rest of the day I stayed away from Larry. A cage of resentment trapped me inside. Even though I had let myself in and closed the door with a loud metallic clang, the sign outside read, "Courtesy of Larry."

The next morning, the thick-barred cage still enclosed me. As I rushed around getting ready for the picnic, Larry wrestled with Darcy on the couch. Her cries of delight irked me. *He gives her attention. Why doesn't he give some to me? He says he loves me but he won't even come to the picnic.* The cage whispered, "Oh, look at him. What a pittance of attention he gives. I bet now he feels like he's such a great dad. What a farce."

Larry and Darcy's continued roughhousing drove me to keep busy preparing the macaroni salad and forming the hamburger patties. I was glad I could bustle around packing diapers and clothes for the kids.

When Larry stood ready to leave, he picked up Darcy, hugging and kissing her. Standing nearby, I waited for him to reach over and kiss me. When he walked out the door with only a "Bye, Kath, see you this afternoon," I silently walked away.

"Darcy, come into your bedroom to dress," I yelled. "We only have a few minutes before we must leave." Noticing the pile of unfolded clothes and the dirty breakfast dishes, I felt the wheels within me turn faster. I rushed about in a futile attempt to slow down time.

Entering her room, I yelled louder. "Darcy, I said come into your bedroom."

She ran into her room and jerked open a drawer, flinging out an old playsuit. "Me wear this!"

I groaned. "But honey, that is all stained. Look at this nice new outfit I bought you. It has a cute bear on it."

She shook her head back and forth, loosening the barrettes I had put in so carefully earlier.

"Stop it! Your barrettes are going to come out. Now look, you can't wear that. It looks dirty. Come over here right now and I'll put this on you. Right now!"

Darcy threw the clothes I handed her onto the floor and jumped up and down, screaming. Her crying grated on my nerves. It seemed as if she were saying, "I have a need and you aren't meeting it. You are a bad mother."

When I couldn't stand it any longer, I barked, "Darcy, stop it right now. I'm telling you you'll wear this outfit. I'm going to get the spoon. Now stop it!"

Thinking I would move past her to get the spoon in the kitchen, I stood up. Instead of taking a step, my hands jerked toward her throat, tightening around her neck. "You look like your father and you're just as obnoxious," I screamed.

In that instant, it was as if I left my body and watched a hysterical woman choking a little girl. The shock left me breathless and I let go.

Darcy crumpled to the floor, crying out in fear and pain. My anger rose again. I grabbed her shoulders hard, hissing, "I'm sick and tired of your temper tantrums and crying. That's all you ever do." I continued to verbally assault her, letting all my frustrations and hate pour out.

In an instant, horror replaced my ebbing anger as I realized what I'd done. I burst into tears and knelt beside Darcy as she sobbed.

"Oh, God, what in the world have I done? God, God where are you? Please help me. I've been doing so well, why can't I cope now? When am I going to be able to control myself?"

Larry's gun flashed through my mind. "I might as well kill myself. I'm no good to anyone. I'm destroying her ... and myself," I sobbed.

I ran down the hall to our room and jerked open the top dresser drawer. The gun seemed to beckon me, sneered, "If you don't take your life, you're going to kill Darcy. There's no hope for you." *It's true! It's true! It's just a matter of time!*

As I reached in for it, another thought intruded. "But what will people think of Jesus if they hear Kathy Miller has taken her life."

"Oh! I don't care about my reputation but I do Jesus's. But, God, what if I kill her in my next rage?"

No voice answered me, but I heard Darcy hysterically sobbing in her bedroom. I closed the drawer and felt like I was slinking in shame down the hall. When I peeked into the room, Darcy saw me and retreated into the corner of her bed up against the wall, looking terrified.

My heart broke and I barely had enough strength to walk over to her. "Honey, I'm so sorry. I don't know what's wrong with me. I can't seem to help myself. I was so wrong. Mommy is wrong. Please forgive me." I tried to gather her into my arms, but she felt stiff. My hot tears dropped onto her head and I could only rock her back and forth. "Oh, God, what should I do? I've got to change."

I didn't want to see Darcy's tear-filled face. Avoiding eye contact, I lifted her to her feet, and explained, "We've got to hurry now." I dressed her in the new outfit. She didn't complain.

In a blur of agony, trying not to think, I gathered everything together and packed the picnic supplies into the car. Wiping my tear-covered face as we drove down the street, I tried not to look back at Darcy sitting silently in her car seat.

We arrived at the park and I attempted to smile as friends greeted me. Remaining on the verge of tears, I was panicked someone might comment about my pained look. *Why did I come? Why do I think*

I have to come? What is wrong with me? I spread a blanket for us to sit on and vaguely noticed the clear blue sky and the warm, leaf-rustling breeze. My depressed spirits contrasted with the beautiful summer California day. Some families around me visited with friends or played softball. Others prepared grills for barbecuing. Darcy excitedly ran to the nearby playground while I settled Mark on the blanket.

I squeezed the last hot tears out of my eyes, embarrassed lest anyone see them. Watching the other families happily playing together drove a knife through my heart. The struggle within me was a waging war. *Larry shouldn't have left that gun. It's his fault I overreacted. If he had stayed to help me, I wouldn't have choked her or thought of suicide.* I wanted to forget what I'd done and accept Larry as he was, but on the other hand, I wanted him to be the husband I needed.

Why isn't Larry here? Doesn't he love me and his family? Sometimes I hate him. For sure, I hate myself and what I've done. I can't ask your forgiveness, Lord, I'm so ashamed. How can I call myself a Christian? I've hurt Darcy so many times, and I'm afraid I'll do it again.

Hopelessness consumed my icy heart. The breeze warmed my body but not my soul. Would anyone be sad if I killed myself? I didn't think so—not if they knew the real me, the angry me.

CHAPTER 11

CONFESSION

June 10

Saturday and Sunday passed without my acknowledgement. Sinking in a quagmire of depression, I didn't want to face the fact I was regressing. In fear of hurting Darcy again, I tried to avert any conflicts with Darcy or Larry.

At the women's neighborhood Bible study Sally briefly commented on my gloominess, but I told her I didn't feel well. When she invited me over on Wednesday afternoon to talk about our next set of lessons, I apprehensively wondered if she would try to delve into the reasons for my sullenness. But I assured myself she sincerely wanted to plan for the next session. How thankful I was she was helping me guide the Bible study until Mark was older and I could take responsibility for leading it again.

On Wednesday afternoon, pushing Mark in his stroller and Darcy dressed in shorts on the warm June day, we walked down the block to Sally's house. With each step more fear swelled within me. *She suspects something wrong, I know it.* But how could she? The burden I carried was overwhelming, but unknown to others. *And no one will ever know it, God. Don't you even try to let others know.* I suspected everyone looked at me with suspicious stares, talking about me behind their backs. A part of me dreaded, yet another part hoped, for a confrontation with Sally. But the thought of a glimmer of hope at the end of a very long train tunnel seemed impossible.

Dressed in jeans and a tailored blue blouse, Sally answered the door in her usual cheerful manner. After leading me into her lovely decorated living room, she brought out toys for Mark and Darcy. Then we chatted as she fixed iced tea. Her bright green eyes sparkled at me, and she smiled with a joy in the Lord I envied.

I loved to come to Sally's house. I felt peaceful just being there. I could tell her kids were older because her house was so clean and ordered. Her uncluttered kitchen counter was wiped clean of any crumbs from her two sons' breakfast. It looked like she had just vacuumed her carpet—there was even a pattern showing where the vacuum had been. I couldn't remember the last time I'd vacuumed or had an uncluttered kitchen counter.

"Well, Kathy," she interrupted my thoughts as she set my glass of tea on the coffee table, "have you thought any more about what we might want to study next session? We've got a couple of weeks to order the materials."

We talked about potential topics, then our conversation drifted to our children after Sally's sons wandered into the room with a balloon. Darcy batted the balloon back and forth, almost tripping over herself and the furniture trying to prevent the boys from hitting it. Perplexed by the strange yellow floating ball bouncing off his nose, Mark laughed in delight.

"Wow, Kathy, I don't think I've ever seen Darcy so animated."

"Are you kidding? She always has that much energy—even more."

"She must be quite a handful. I remember Shawn had that much energy but Bryan seemed a little calmer. It seems like God usually gives us children with different personalities. Is Mark calmer or more active than Darcy?"

"Oh, Mark is definitely calmer. He's my little sweetheart. He's so easy to care for. I sure wish Darcy were like him. God knew I sure needed him easier to care for. Sometimes, I can get so mad at Darcy ..." My palms grew wet and clammy. My voice trailed off, knowing I had revealed too much.

I can't tell Sally. I'm sure she has never been so angry with her boys she wanted to kill them.

My face flushed and I glanced toward Sally, expecting a reproof. Maybe some Bible verse quoted at me, or at the least some sort of disapproval. She intently yet seemingly gently looked at me, waiting for me to finish. "Oh, sometimes Darcy really gets on my nerves," I blurted out.

In a second, I flashed back to the time a month earlier I'd shared with another friend how frustrated I could become. She seemed shocked and quickly changed the subject. It was obvious she looked down on me. Certainly, the same thing would happen now. Maybe Sally would feel forced to tell me I couldn't help her lead the study anymore. Inwardly, I cringed and turned my head away, as tears threatened to build up against my eyelids.

When I peeked back, Sally continued to gaze at me as if I had something more to say. *I wish she wouldn't look at me like that. She won't understand.* But my heart wanted the polluted flood waters, which thrust against my emotional dam, to be released so the reservoir might be refilled with clean, clear spring water. Stinging tears succeeded in pushing their way to the surface and spilled over.

I quickly wiped my eyes as if an eyelash were creating it. *But if I don't tell someone, I'm going to explode. I don't want to hurt Darcy again.*

"Well," I hesitantly began, "Darcy gets to me sometimes and I have a hard time controlling my temper. Sometimes I'm afraid I'm going to hurt her. I've taken my anger out on her in some terrible ways."

There, I had said it! The horrible truth was out.

Afraid to confront Sally's condemning look, I glanced the other way. When she started to speak, I cringed. *Here it comes, I knew I shouldn't have said anything.*

"Yes, I bet Darcy is a challenge. My Shawn was more like Darcy. Wow, he could frustrate me. I remember feeling so angry with him one time I shook him by the shoulders until his teeth clattered. Those were some very difficult times."

I turned my head toward her, my mouth dropping open. "What? You're kidding. You would get frustrated? I wouldn't have thought you'd do something like that."

Sally laughed. "Oh sure. I think most mothers feel a kind of rage—or out of control frustration—at one time or another. I certainly hope I'm not the only one. Kids can be hard to handle. Mothering is the hardest job on earth as far as I'm concerned, even more than marriage."

Relief flooded me. Sighing, I thought, "I'm not the only mother who feels angry. I'm not alone. Oh, thank you, Jesus. Thank you."

When I finally could hold back the tears, I asked, "Sally, what do you find helps you when you feel angry at the boys?"

"Well, I certainly don't have a formula but … hmm … let me think. Maybe being aware of when I'm under extra stress helps. My body often tells me through sore muscles or headaches I'm too tense."

But does she really understand what I'm talking about—the degree? Does she realize what I'm afraid to say? I don't know, but it doesn't matter. She feels strong anger, too. "Oh, okay. Now that I think of it, I have a tendency to grit my teeth when I start to get angry. I guess that could be a prompt to ask God to help me."

"Since you recognize that, try to distract yourself from your anger when you begin to grit your teeth."

"What do you mean by distract?"

"Personally, I've noticed frustration gives me lots of energy so I will pound a pillow or run in place. Just do something to relieve the pressure and give yourself breathing space so you can think about the real cause of your anger. You see, most of the time when I'm angry at Shawn, I'm not only angry at him, but other things—like Gary. It's because I'm not trusting God for the situation or person. I really believe the bottom line of coping with my stress and anger is completely trusting God is in control of my life. That means even when Gary or another person doesn't do what I think they should. The challenge is to let God have his way even if it seems to spell disaster."

I knew she was right. I wasn't trusting the Lord for my marriage or submitting to his plan for me as a mother. I usually blamed Larry and the kids for my anger, and was bitter toward Larry and God for my discontent.

I felt hesitant to tell Sally about the unhappiness I felt in my marriage but since I'd already said so much, I smiled in embarrassment and said, "I'm so mad at Larry, I know I'm not trusting God for my marriage. Would you pray for me right now God will heal our marriage and heal me from my anger? I've prayed about it for a long time by myself but I can't seem to get control. Maybe if you pray with me, the Lord will perform a miracle."

Sally nodded. "Of course, I'll pray for you. I'll pray every day the Lord will reveal what the root of the problem is so that you can dig it out and expose it. And remember, don't be too hard on yourself. God knows you can't be perfect here on earth, so don't expect that of yourself. Only Jesus is perfect. We're still in the process of growing. When you feel really uptight or angry, give me a call and we'll talk about it. Let's pray right now."

As Sally prayed, I felt strengthened ... and also challenged. *Could I really trust God's plan even if it wasn't all I wanted?*

When she finished, I thanked her. As we talked for a few minutes longer, I felt like bursting with joy. As I walked the kids home, I mused, *I revealed my horrible secret and Sally didn't condemn me or even react with shock. She understood. She still respects me as a person and as a Christian. Will her support and prayers be the answer? Oh, God, yes, I hope so. How I want this to be the end of my awful nightmare.*

During the next few days and into the weekend, the burden of my anger was gone. I remembered to discipline Darcy consistently and whenever I sensed I was tired, I took a nap while the kids napped. Sometimes, I called Sally to share my pressures; other times, I jogged in place. More and more often, I could recognize the beginning stages of my anger. My rested, peaceful soul rejoiced in the Lord and I knew Sally's prayers—and mine—were being answered.

At the next Bible study the following Monday, I sensed the Lord prompting me to ask my friends to pray for me and for the solution to my anger. *But Lord, I don't need any more prayer. Sally is praying for me and I've been doing fantastic. Everything's okay now.*

But the urging continued even though I tried to ignore it. At the end of the Bible study, when Sally asked if there were any prayer requests, I blurted out, "Yes, I have one."

Feeling my face redden, I frantically tried to think of something else for which I could ask prayer. When my mind went blank, I stared at Sally. She smiled reassuringly.

Okay, Lord, if you want me to, I will.

Taking a deep breath, but speaking only slightly more than a whisper with my head lowered, I said, "Well, I wanted to ask … uh … to ask all of you to pray for me and … " I gulped and tried to still my furiously beating heart, "…uh … my anger toward Darcy. I've been getting awfully angry at her lately and I'm having a hard time coping."

I could feel Sally silently cheering me on. But then Julie giggled and spoke up, "Oh, Kathy, I'm sure it's not really as bad as you think. Everyone gets angry. You're the last person who needs prayer for that. You're always so calm and cool with Darcy and Mark."

"Yes, Kathy," Mary continued, "I'm sure it can't be that bad. We all get upset with our kids—everybody does. I'm sure you're making a big thing out of nothing."

Frustrated, I looked around trying to formulate my thoughts into words. "No, really, I need your prayers. It's been pretty tough almost the whole past year, and I'm scared. I can't seem to grasp the Lord's power in this area of my life. Darcy gets to me too easily."

By now, everyone's sober faces had riveted on me. Julie spoke first. "I'm really sorry I laughed, Kathy. I just didn't take you seriously at first. But I'll remember to pray for you every day. I know the Lord will strengthen you."

"Thank you, Julie. I really appreciate everyone's prayers."

The tension in my chest subsided as the seven women nodded their heads, agreeing to pray for me. Then during the closing prayer, each one mentioned me in her prayer. I felt humbled but hopeful. *Will their support really help? Oh, Lord, please make a difference.*

After Sally dismissed us, I felt awkward walking with everyone to get the children. Then Julie spoke up again. "Kathy, I've discovered if I don't try to deny my anger when I first feel it, I can face it and deal with it better. Saying I'm not starting to feel angry only makes it fester within me."

"Yes, I agree," Mary joined in. "I've also heard we should communicate our anger through 'I' messages instead of 'you' messages."

"Oh, okay. But what does that mean?"

"Well, 'I' messages are phrases like, 'I feel angry when that happens.' But, 'you' messages are words blaming someone like, 'you make me angry.' If I explain to Brad how I feel instead of blaming him, he seems less likely to become defensive about what I'm saying. And I have opened the door for better understanding and acceptance of my anger. I can't say it works all the time with him but I have seen an improvement in the way we relate."

I nodded my head. I didn't completely understand all she meant but I was beginning to see there was a lot I needed to learn.

Then Pat spoke up and shared a time when she had become angry with her daughter and I could see they were really trying to help. The Lord did want me to share my experience. He was going to use everyone's prayers and advice.

When we reached the house where the children were being cared for, I opened the door and saw Darcy playing on the floor with blocks. She saw me and raced to me, hugging my legs. Full of hope, I lifted her into the air and kissed her. "Darcy," I whispered, "I love you and from now on things are going to be great."

For the first time there was a tiny light at the end of the long train tunnel. As I walked with Darcy and Mark, I remembered a verse I hadn't thought of for a long time. I couldn't remember the exact words so when I got home, I flipped my Bible open and found James 5:16. I read out loud, "Therefore, confess your sins to one another and pray for one another, that you may be healed. The prayer of a righteous person has great power as it is working."

Thank you, Lord, for a caring group who loves me exactly the way I need. Maybe there is hope after all.

CHAPTER 12

CELEBRATE!

June 20

"Honey, this is a really nice restaurant. I'm so glad we came here." I don't know why but I'd been surprised Larry had chosen so generously.

"I thought you would enjoy it. After all, it's not every day we get to celebrate our seventh anniversary. Happy anniversary!" Larry raised his water goblet into the air. I lifted mine to meet his, gently clinking them together in a toast.

Seven years before, June 20, 1970, we were married. I could hardly believe it. I scanned the restaurant noticing the antiques and old-fashioned decor which enhanced the romantic and nostalgic atmosphere. I watched Larry sitting across from me, peacefully enjoying his gourmet dinner of crab. As I savored my prime rib, I mused over the ten years since I'd met Larry at a high school water polo game.

"Do you know what the most significant part of our history together is for me?" I reflected out loud. "It is how the Lord used you to bring me to him. If you hadn't taken me to your church, I might not have heard Jesus wanted me to know him personally. Thank you, honey."

Larry's grin caused a flood of emotions to well up within me. It was the same easy-going smile I remembered from our courting days making me feel so special. My insecurity had thirsted for his love and acceptance. A guy had actually accepted me just as I was. I began to feel the joy of stability and love. Then I remembered it was seven years later and the familiar, tormenting loneliness of the present brought me back to reality.

If Larry really loves me like he says he does, why doesn't he spend more time with me? Oh sure, it's easy for him to take me out for our anniversary, it's only once a year, but what about the way he treats me on the other days of the year?

The insecurity and loneliness I experienced before I met Larry returned. *See? He really never loved me to begin with.*

Larry broke into my thoughts. "Sweetie, you look so sad. What are you thinking about?"

Pushing my creamed peas around on my plate, I stammered, "Oh, I was just thinking ... about ... uh ... how you met so many of my needs when we were dating."

"Well, don't I meet them now too?" he laughed.

I tried to laugh. "Well, I *would* love for you to spend more time with me."

Larry's smile faded. "Oh, that again. I've told you I'm trying to gain financial security for our family which means I need to work longer hours. Believe me, it'll pay off in the end. You'll see."

My chest tightened in a familiar way I recognized tension and stress these days. "Sweetheart, I know you want to do that. But I would rather have you around, not money. I want *you*."

Larry rolled his eyes upward. "You just don't understand. I've explained it to you before."

Oh, no, now we're going to argue on our anniversary. Boy, did I say the wrong thing. How can I put my feelings into an "I" message? But rather than risking the possibility of saying the wrong thing again, I desperately tried to find something else to talk about.

"Have you noticed how Mark is sitting up for a few seconds already? Hard to believe he's almost seven months old. " I tried to giggle. "He's such a good baby. Hope he lives through Darcy picking on him."

Larry's effort to laugh at the changed subject made me realize the argument had been dropped. We were at a truce again, but it felt like we both stood on the edge of a precipice and any gust of wind could blow us over into the abyss.

For the rest of the evening, we skirted the issue of Larry's long working hours. Instead, we chatted about our upcoming birthdays. We were only four days apart--four days after our anniversary. At least we could talk about the family birthday party my mother was planning for next Friday.

On Friday afternoon, I was excited about the party. Evidently, Darcy sensed the excitement too, because she wouldn't stay in bed for her nap.

"Darcy, we're going to be up late tonight at the birthday party. You've got to go to sleep."

I walked her back to her bedroom. "Mommy, I not tired. I want to play," she whined.

"Now, don't start whining," I commanded her, my voice rising. "Please, Darcy, try to sleep. You'll be happier tonight if you're rested. Now, just lie there and try."

I walked out of her room sensing worry was eroding my trust in God's plan. In my mind there just was no way her not sleeping could be a good plan. If that was what God wanted, he didn't know much. I smiled to myself with such an irreverent thought but it really was the truth. *Lord, if she doesn't sleep, she's going to be a brat tonight. I don't want to have to come home early. Father, please help her to go to sleep.*

I had barely walked into the kitchen and begun wiping the counter when Darcy appeared at the doorway again. I gasped, "Darcy, you aren't even trying. Now get back in your bed, right now!" My facial muscles contorted into a fierce scowl. Opening her eyes wide, she turned abruptly and ran into her bedroom crying.

Oh, that girl. Why doesn't she cooperate? I just don't understand why she can't lie still in that bed for even one minute.

Suddenly, the heat of the day and tension in my body swallowed my patience. I couldn't stand it. I rushed into the bedroom and undressed. Beads of sweat clung to my body. I quickly pulled on my bathing suit and ran to the backyard. I felt like screaming.

I dove into the pool and the cool water cleansed my body of tension and frustration. As I swam several laps, my tears mingled with the water. *Jesus, Jesus, please make Darcy go to sleep. When she doesn't take a nap, she cries and whines. I want to have a good time at the party. After all, I'm the birthday girl.*

I climbed onto an air mattress and floated peacefully under the cloudless, blue sky. Kicking gently, I guided the raft around the pool, trailing my hands in the refreshing, sparkling water.

My thoughts wandered back to Larry and our discussion at the restaurant. *Lord, why can't I just love and accept Larry as he is? I'm always trying to change him, but it doesn't do any good. I want him to spend more time with me. I want him to talk to me more, but my nagging only pushes him farther away. Jesus, I really believe you want to make him into your kind of man, but it's not happening.*

An inner voice rebuffed me. "My thoughts are not your thoughts, neither are your ways my ways … For as the heavens are higher than the earth, so are my ways higher than your ways, and my thoughts than your thoughts."

Yes, Lord, I know those verses from Isaiah 55, but you still aren't doing anything. Is my nagging in the way? Is that it?

He didn't have to answer me because it knew it was. No matter how hard I tried to have kind, loving communication, invariably negative, pessimistic nagging would win over.

"Lord, I just don't feel loved. I know you love me …" I tried to clarify my thoughts "… but with the way I treat Darcy and Larry, I guess I find it hard to believe you can love me. Oh, I know about your unconditional love but I don't feel it."

Tears trickled down my temples into my wet hair. *Father, I really do want to love Larry and Darcy unconditionally. I just don't seem to know how.*

I paused as if expecting a sermon on love. But instead, three words echoed in my head: "Show your love."

Show my love … show my love. The words ricocheted in my mind. I thought of many ways to demonstrate love but set them aside one by one, hoping for an unusual, spectacular way. Then it occurred to me: *I'll have a surprise birthday party for Larry. I've never done that before. I'll show him how much I love him and he'll have to love me back. Yeah, he'll be so grateful he'll have to spend more time with me. That's it.*

I paddled over to the side and climbed out of the pool. Wrapping a towel around me, I breezed into the house and down the hall, formulating the list of people I would invite.

Passing Darcy's room, I glanced in, expecting to find her playing. I stopped. She lay on her bed, surrounded by books … asleep.

"Praise you, Lord. Oh, Father, I really appreciate you doing that for me. You showed me your love, now I'm going to show Larry mine."

I didn't want to admit to myself my motives were mixed. *Since I've always wanted a surprise birthday party, he must want that too. It's going to be so fun. Wait until he walks in the door.* I tried to push away the niggling thought, "But Larry doesn't like parties, especially focused on him." *Oh, who doesn't like to be focused on. That's silly. He's going to love it.*

CHAPTER 13

SURPRISE PARTY

June 25

"Yes, Claudia, that's right. The party is this Saturday. I'm glad you can come." I was relieved Claudia had called to let me know the invitation had arrived safely. I hoped I hadn't forgotten anyone.

"Kathy, how are you going to make the party a surprise if you're having it at your house?"

"That's the best part. I had Jim ask Larry to play tennis with him in the afternoon. Everyone will arrive here at 2:30 and Jim will bring him back at three. Doesn't that sound great? I'm so excited. You know, I've never done anything like this before. I sure hope it works."

"Well, it sounds foolproof to me. I just hope Larry feels like playing tennis that day."

"That's the least of my worries. Larry will play tennis any chance he gets. What he may not like, though, is coming home all sweaty and tired to find twenty people waiting for him. And guess what? I'm going to have a casket here."

"What?"

"Yes, a casket. Connie's husband made a wooden casket for a Halloween party they had and he's bringing it with them. Can you believe that?"

"That is hilarious. Wow. Maybe you can get him to lay down in it."

"I'm not counting on that, but we'll see. That would be fabulous, though. Hey, gotta go. Still have lots to do. See you Saturday."

I hung up smiling. *This is going to be so much fun. I just can't wait to see his face. If this doesn't earn his love, nothing will.*

During the next few days, Darcy really got on my nerves. I had so much to think about and organize, and she seemed to sense my tension, demanding even more attention from me than usual. As I tried to plan the menu, she wanted to play with modeling clay, which I knew would make a big mess. But I also knew saying no would elicit persistent begging and a temper tantrum. I was not prepared to handle that, so I retrieved the clay, set it out on the table, and reminded Darcy of the rules for using it.

In the meantime, my mind swirled with plans. *I'll make the cake on Friday night while Larry is at work. Sally can keep it at her house until the next day. But where am I going to hide all the extra food and paper goods? I don't have enough cabinet space in the kitchen.*

I tried to think of all the other places in the house where Larry seldom looked, possible hiding places, and I decided which of those I could use. Now I was more confident. I was determined to pull this surprise off, hoping it would make Larry appreciate me more.

On Saturday morning, I could barely sit still. I tried to keep busy cleaning the house. But Darcy and even Mark seemed to sense my nervousness, whining and crying for attention.

"Darcy, please let me get the house clean," I pleaded. It would be so embarrassing to let people see my messiness and dirty floors. Finally, the house was beginning to look better and I hoped Larry hadn't noticed my unusual furious pace. Once he left at one o'clock, I would have to put the kids down for their naps, take all the food out, wrap his gift, and get the cake from Sally's house. Internally, I felt as if I were a rubber band pulled taut to its limit. Nothing could go wrong. This party had to come off perfectly.

I flashed back to another surprise I had pulled on Larry when we were first dating in high school. After school one day, when I knew he was practicing with his water polo team at a nearby college, I drove over and walked right into the pool area waving at Larry. He turned crimson as all his friends teased him because girlfriends never went to practices. I watched from a nearby bench for about twenty minutes and was the only spectator around. I was delighted when his buddies needled him for several days after that. Boy, that was fun. After that happened, Larry kept telling me I shouldn't do it again. But I could tell by his smile he halfway enjoyed the attention.

Larry's voice broke through my reverie. "Kathy, Jim's here. We're going now."

"Okay, have a good time." I cried out from the back bedroom. Little did he know what he would be coming home to. Now it was time to really get busy.

I picked up Mark and could smell his diaper. I had changed him just thirty minutes before but now I'd be delayed even if only for a few moments. I had no time to spare. Taking the opportunity to review mentally my "To-Do" list, I pulled a clean diaper out of the drawer and changed him again.

Distracted by thoughts of what still needed done, I nervously laid Mark in his crib and shut the door. *Whew, that's one thing settled.* I sighed. But I was only two steps down the hall when I heard him start to cry. *That's funny. He usually goes right to sleep.*

I walked back into his room and checked his diaper pins but didn't find anything wrong. I laid him down again. He began to cry immediately. "No, Mark, don't do this to me. You're my good baby. Go to sleep."

I closed the door, hoping being out of his sight would stop his crying. He continued at full volume. *If I get him up, I won't be able to do as much as I would otherwise. He's got to go to sleep.*

I decided to put Darcy down for her nap and wait to see if Mark would stop crying. After I raced through reading a book to her, Darcy wiggled on top of her bed. "Mommy, can we swim later?"

"No, honey, we're going to have company this afternoon. Now, Mommy really needs you to help and go to sleep, okay?"

"Goody, goody. Who coming?"

She began her habit of a thousand questions I had no time for. I raised my voice to make my point for her to sleep and closed the door behind me. My heart sank as I heard Mark still screaming. *I can't let him scream like that. It drives me crazy and will keep Darcy awake. Maybe I can rock him to sleep.*

While rocking him I concentrated on all the things I still needed to do. *Oh, no, it's 1:30. I've got to hurry.* I was one blink away from tears as Darcy's door creaked open. Watching her disappear into the kitchen, I sighed, "All right, Lord. I'll just ignore her for now. It's more important Mark goes to sleep."

Mark's alert eyes stared at me. "For God's sake, Mark," I whispered, "go to sleep." I rocked faster. I tried to sing but my throat was too tight. Finally after fifteen minutes, Mark's heavy eyelids closed and I laid him carefully in his crib. "Don't come in now, Darcy. Just stay away."

Tiptoeing out of the room, I practically ran down the hall wondering where Darcy could be. The minutes were fast disappearing and the guests would start to arrive soon.

I rushed into the kitchen to continue working. I gasped when I saw Darcy sitting on the tile surrounded by hundreds of tiny pieces of modeling clay. "Oh no, why did I leave that out on the table?"

In one stride, I stood towering over Darcy. "Oh, damn. Look what you've done. I've got too many things to do without having to clean up that mess."

I raised my hand and shot it down, slapping Darcy's cheek. She covered her face with her hands and screamed hysterically. "I don't care if you cry all day. I need to get too much ready! Can't you ever do anything right?"

I don't care. She's caused me trouble just when I need all the help I can get. Now, nothing will be ready.

By the time I'd picked up most of the mess, my anger had seeped out of me and Darcy's tear-filled face crushed my heart. The slapping sound echoed within me. Guilt replaced my fury. "Oh, God, I've done it again. I wanted everything to be perfect and now I've spoiled it. Look what I've done to Darcy. Is there no hope for me? Please help me! I've been so patient lately. I thought I was over this."

Darcy stared at me as tears continued to roll down her cheeks. As I started to move toward her, she again covered her face. I took a deep breath, then let it out slowly.

"Darcy, I'm sorry. I'm really sorry. Mommy wants to get everything ready for the party and you made a mess. I shouldn't have gotten mad at you, though."

I gently pulled her hands down from her face and tried to smile. "C'mon now, please help me get ready, then we'll go over to Sally's house and get Daddy's cake."

Her face brightened. "Cake? Okay."

The red mark on her cheek seemed to be fading to a dull blush. *Father, I promise never to touch Darcy again in anger. I'm sorry.*

Sniffing back my tears, I grasped Darcy's hand and headed to Sally's to retrieve the cake. My shame covered me like a water-soaked blanket and I couldn't even look at Darcy, much less apologize again.

Shortly after we returned and I had just taken out the chips and dips, the guests started arriving. Several of our friends helped me set out the food, and at 2:50, I stationed one of the men at the window to look for Jim's car.

At 3:05 he yelled, "Here they come."

Everyone took their preassigned places. Smiling and giggling excitedly, they kept whispering, "Shhh," making more noise than before.

Suddenly, I remembered the movie camera. I ran down the hall, retrieved it, and stood ready.

Larry opened the door. His wet T-shirt was clinging to his skin and his hair was disheveled. He look tired.

Everyone shouted, "Surprise!" and started singing "Happy birthday to you …"

Larry blinked. He stood with his mouth open, his hand still on the doorknob. He stared as everyone broke into laughter.

Larry's wide-eyed amazement broke into a half-smile. "Oh no, I can't believe it. You've got to be kidding."

He stepped over to the nearest chair and plopped down. I laid my hand on his shoulder and leaned over to kiss him. "Happy birthday, sweetheart. I love you."

"Oh, honey, this is fantastic. How did you ever do it?"

"Not very easily," I joked, but I knew the price had been high--too high.

Everyone surrounded Larry and congratulated him on his twenty-eighth birthday. Screeching her delight, Darcy ran over and jumped onto his lap.

Father, thank you everything went so well—except for my outburst at Darcy. My heart was heavy. It wasn't the sweet victory I'd expected. It showed me I wasn't handling stress as well as I thought. I could see the battle was yet to be won.

CHAPTER 14

LOVE IS ...

July 10

"Honey, I just have to thank you again for the wonderful surprise party. That was something else. You really did surprise me." Larry wrapped his arms around me, squeezing tightly.

"I was really excited planning it," I said, returning his smile. "Just wait until you see the movies of you walking in the door. You won't believe the amazed look on your face."

But Larry's appreciative words weren't what I really wanted. Had he spent more time with me this week? No. He had been just as consumed by his work as usual. What did I have to do to get his attention anyway? Kill myself?

When Agnes and Neil's invitation came a week later inviting us to a neighborhood barbecue, I thought, *This will be Larry's opportunity to show me how appreciative he is.*

"Larry, did you notice Agnes and Neil's invitation to their house for Saturday?" I anxiously inquired.

"Yes, I did. Unfortunately, I already told Steve I'd work to repay him for a time he worked for me. I'm really sad I have to miss it."

I turned away disappointed. *Now, Kathy, don't get upset. He didn't do it on purpose; it just happened. Don't blame him; it's not his fault.* Even though I realized it wasn't his choice to work, I wanted to blame him. *But why does this always happen?*

When Saturday arrived, Larry got ready to leave. Walking over to me, he commented, "Honey, I'm really sorry I can't go to the barbecue with you. It sounds like a lot of fun and I would have enjoyed being with you and the kids."

I stared straight into his eyes. "Really, Larry? Do you mean that? You really would have gone if it hadn't been for your promise to Steve?"

Larry appeared surprised at my intensity. "Of course, Kathy. Don't you think I want to go?"

My mind raced. *I don't want to get into another argument. How can I share my feelings without complaining?*

"Well, it's just I miss you so much and it *seems like*—you'll notice, I said seems like—every time there is something to do, you have to work. I just wonder sometimes if you even want to be with me and the kids."

Larry's hazel eyes softened. "I'm sorry I give you that impression. But I assure you I really do want to be with you. As soon as we get on our feet financially, I'll have more time to spend with you. I promise."

For the first time, I believed him. He really did want to be with us. *Maybe he means it this time, but what about next time?* I wasn't ready to entrust my heart completely. Danger of being hurt still seemed to lurk behind his inviting behavior.

A couple of hours later, Darcy, Mark, and I walked over to Agnes and Neil's backyard where several families mingled. Agnes had prepared four large salads and the barbecue coals were hot-white, ready to cook hamburgers and hot dogs.

Several of the neighbors sat in groups visiting, while children ran back and forth chasing balls and playing with the dog.

"Wow, Agnes, this is really special. But I still can't believe you wouldn't let me bring any food."

Agnes grinned. "Well, we just wanted everyone to come, have a good time, and not worry about anything."

"That's really sweet of you. Looks like you've got a good turnout."

I scanned the backyard. Noticing Pat and Sally talking together, I walked over to them. Darcy trailed behind me, fearfully eyeing the dog, and Mark took in the view as I balanced him on my hip.

Once Darcy became acquainted with the dog, she raced around with the other children. I watched her play. She looked so darling in her clean, green-and-white-checked shorts outfit. Her blonde, short hair actually looked as if it were starting to get thicker. She was growing up so fast.

When it was time to eat, I prepared our plates and sat down beside Ted, one of our neighbors. Moving over to make room for us on the picnic bench, he helped me set down the glasses of punch.

Darcy immediately chomped on her hot dog. *No wonder she's hungry, she ran around like crazy.*

Ted brushed Darcy's bangs back from her sweaty forehead. "Darcy, you're so cute and such a good little girl."

Pride welled up within me. "Yes, Darcy is a good little girl. Although she does sometimes remind me of the little girl in the nursery rhyme who when she was good was very, very good, but when she was bad, she was horrid."

Ted laughed.

"Darcy's my special little girl." I hugged her, kissing Darcy on the top of her head. The love I felt at that moment brought tears to my eyes. *I really do love you, Darcy.*

But by the time I had thought the words, confusion and guilt surrounded the warm feelings of love and suffocated them. Guilt snickered, *How can you say you love her when you treat her so badly?* Confusion stabbed, *What kind of love hits and kicks and slaps and ...*

Trying to numb the pain in my heart, I turned to Ted. "I hear you landed a new job. How's it going?"

As Ted raved about his higher paying position, my imagination continued its dialogue. *I'm trying. I'm trying. I do love Darcy.*

"When she's good," the voice argued. "What kind of love is that?"

Why do I hate her so much when she's naughty? Can love exist alongside hate?

Then a long lost memory surfaced of attending a conference where the speaker said, "Love is a choice for the highest good of the person."

That's the answer. Love is a choice, not a feeling. I do love Darcy. I just have to learn to express my love in choices for her good.

The condemning voices seemed to retreat. I remembered the many ways I had hurt Darcy and as Ted continued to talk about his new job, I mused, *I am doing better. I'm not getting angry as often. God is working. I just have to continue to trust him. And that's that!*

Later, sitting around a picnic table, I visited with several neighbors who were in the Bible study. Mary asked, "Kathy, how are you doing controlling your anger? I've been praying for you."

"Well, uh ..." I forced a smile and my face grew hot. "I have my ups and downs. I guess I have the hardest times when Darcy makes mistakes. She does so many dumb things."

"Kathy, I think that's because she's a child," Julie spoke up.

"Yea, I know," I replied, "but it's so aggravating."

"I agree, Kathy," Mary said. "I did something once which helped me along those lines. Using the information I found in a child development book, I made a list of everything a child Jeremy's age might do, like spill milk, or not pick up his toys, or not share—things like that. I put the list on the refrigerator and instead of getting angry, I put a check mark beside the behavior. It really helped me remember his immaturity caused him to act like that. I still gave him consequences so he would learn but I realized he wasn't doing it on purpose. My frustration really subsided."

Everyone murmured their approval.

"Wow, Mary," I whispered as I fought tears. "That's a great idea. I'll do it."

The conversation continued and Julie commented, "I'm so excited. Emily is finally potty trained. It took so long and there were several times I gave up realizing she wasn't ready. My frustration really subsided then."

Julie's news made me think about Darcy. It had been several months since I put her back into diapers. She was over two-and-a-half now. *Maybe it's time to try again.* It sure would be nice to have to only change Mark. And the summer months were supposed to be the easiest time to try because she'd be able to run around in just her training pants.

Later, as I walked home with the kids, I reasoned, "Well, if she doesn't respond right away or I can't handle it, I can always quit. I'm going to do it."

When I made a list of reasonable expectations of Darcy at her age, I added, "Darcy will have lots of potty training accidents."

The next day, I dressed Darcy only in her training pants and reintroduced her to the potty chair. For once I felt more confident of something which would help me. *Thank you, Lord, for guiding me.*

The following day, when Darcy cheerfully instructed Mark how to stack blocks on the family room floor, I grabbed hold of the few minutes of peace to get something accomplished. I began dusting the living room furniture. Suddenly, I sensed words in my heart as real as if they had been spoken out loud.

"Tell Larry you love him."

Where in the world did that come from? God, is that you? Well, if it is, don't hold your breath. I had to laugh thinking of that. *Larry is off on another flying trip today and didn't take me and the kids with him again. Those rotting apple pieces are still stuck on the ceiling and walls of the laundry room and as far as I'm concerned they are the memorial to my rotten marriage you haven't healed. You may be doing a work helping my anger but you haven't done a single thing to change Larry. I haven't said "I love you" for a long time and I don't plan to until he changes.*

I had to chuckle again. Just the other day as Larry walked in from the garage through the laundry room, he pointed to the wall with a confused look and said, "Do you know what these brown pieces are?"

I put on my most innocent look and replied, "No, I don't." I loved the sneaky feeling of knowing something he didn't. I knew full well and enjoyed being reminded of the day I'd knelt by my bed praying for his plane to crash. The plane hadn't crashed, but I could still be angry. It felt satisfying to rehearse Larry's unloving deeds including how the birthday party hadn't made any difference. Each rotten apple piece seemed to represent each of Larry's sins toward me. *He's the rotten guy not me.*

God, I'm not about to say those words because they will give Larry ammunition against me. He'll think I'm approving of his negligence.

I tried to divert my attention back to dusting when the same sensation repeated, "Tell Larry you love him."

God, I can't. I can't let down the guard in my heart. It's just too dangerous. If I soften my heart, he'll stomp on it again and make me feel even more rejected.

Only seconds later, the voice said, "Then think it the next time you see Larry."

"That's very strange, God," I murmured. "What good would that do? He wouldn't even hear me."

A moment of clarity dawned on me. "If he can't hear me then he can't use it against me. Alright, Lord, I'll do it, even if it's not true." My voice turned into a smirk. "I want to be your obedient servant."

But the thought of even thinking the three dangerous words created an energy fueled by fear. For the rest of the day, I felt like I was on some sort of hyper drug. I kept telling myself, "I'm going to do it, I'm going do it. I have to obey God. I have to."

That evening, I heard the garage door go up and the car's engine rumble to a stop. The laundry room door scraped open and I knew Larry was walking through where the rotten apple pieces spoke of his rejection.

Walking down the hall toward him, I commanded myself, "I will think it; I will think it. I will obey God." I stared at him, gulped, and thought, "I love you…" And then the smirk returned and I added, "but I don't really."

Even though I gave him a peck on the cheek, I knew the statement wasn't true. *Lord, I don't think it ever can be.*

CHAPTER 15

SEVEN STEPS

August 1

I glanced at the many rows of book racks and was amazed. *This Christian bookstore has added a lot of books and items since I was here last. How am I ever going to choose a book for Stacy to read in the hospital?*

Then a title in the family section caught my eye. Picking it up, I read *Understanding the Male Temperament*. The author was someone named Tim LaHaye. I laughed. *Boy, could I stand to learn about Larry's temperament.* The more I looked through it, the more interested I became. *Maybe if I understand Larry, I won't always be trying to change him.* I decided I would buy it along with something else for Stacy.

When I finally found a book I thought she would enjoy, I paid for both, and drove home hoping Darcy and Mark would cooperate and let me read later on.

That afternoon, when Darcy and Mark both went down for their naps easily, I praised the Lord. Now I could start my book. Two hours later I was still reading and thrilled the kids were still asleep. Fascinated, I read about the four different temperaments Mr. LaHaye described. I identified Larry's temperament--and mine. *No wonder he reacts the way he does. And no wonder I react the way I do. I've always known Larry doesn't look at things the same way I do, but I've never understood why. Now I know.*

For the next couple of days, I read every spare moment I could. I began to understand my melancholy temperament often resulted in perfectionism. For the first time, I fully acknowledged I did tend to be a perfectionist. I had never recognized how much it influenced so many areas of my life. *Maybe these perfectionistic tendencies are what makes me so impatient and demanding of Darcy. I'll keep an eye on myself and see if it influences the way I treat her.*

I was strangely encouraged and prayed, "Lord, keep showing me what's going on inside me feeding my anger."

Toward the end of the book, there was a section called "How to Cure Anger, Bitterness, or Resentment." I wondered if following its seven steps could help me. A spark of hope lit within my heart as I read the section. *Lord, is this another reason you prompted me to buy this book?*

I read eagerly the first step: "Face your anger as sin." I didn't know if I wanted to call my anger sin all the time. I knew my anger was a habit, a habit often controlling me, taking over my thoughts and actions. That was wrong. "Okay, Father, I'm going to start off on the right foot by telling you I agree my anger habit is wrong, it is sin. Please forgive me."

Okay, good start. Step two was "Confess every angry thought or deed as soon as it occurs." That was interesting because I tended to wait until bedtime to confess my sins from the day. *Following this step will be difficult. And why does the author refer to my thoughts? My anger is caused by outside circumstances and other people. He seems to indicate the cause is internal—my thoughts and perceptions.*

I recalled the last few times I was out of control. Every time had started with not trusting the Lord for the circumstances I was in. Then I became worried or tense and these feelings turned into anger. "Lord, I ask you to help me recognize when I'm starting to think negatively or angrily."

"Ask God to take away this angry pattern" was step three. *Okay, I will again even though I've been begging for almost a year. Here goes. Father, I ask you to take away my angry thought pattern. Even as I ask you my faith is weak. Please help my unbelief.*

Step four said: "Forgive the person who has caused your anger." Darcy! Larry! I was most often angry with them. But forgive *them? Lord, I'm the one who needs forgiveness. I'm the one who is in the wrong.* But I knew I didn't totally believe that. I believed Larry didn't spend enough time with me or have the right priorities. And Darcy demanded too much of my time and energy—too much of *me*. I was bitter toward them and now I could see that at the root of my problem. I had never been honest with myself because I knew as a Christian I shouldn't be bitter.

I guess I am pretty good at denial, eh, Lord? All right, then. I ask you to forgive me for my bitterness and help me forgive them. I know you are using them to make me more of the godly woman you want me to be. I just keep taking this mass of clay off your potter's wheel. Help me stay there!

"Formally give thanks for anything that bothers you," spelled out number five. This was becoming ridiculous. It might take all day to follow through on this step. Everything bothered me. Darcy's wet and dirty training pants, raisins in the rug, Larry working long hours, the dripping faucet Larry hadn't fixed.

As I clicked off in my mind a long list, I realized these were the temptations flaming my anger. These were the potentially dangerous situations I needed to watch for.

I jumped up from the sofa and retrieved a piece of paper and pen, writing them down. I put it beside Darcy's child development list on the refrigerator, alongside the other lists.

I laughed. *My whole life is being shown for the whole world to see, right on my frig.*

Returning to the couch, I read the sixth step: "Think only good, wholesome, and positive thoughts." *Are you kidding me? It feels like there's nothing good about my life.* I knew this step would be difficult. I saw only the negative and found it hard to focus on God's joy when circumstances weren't going my way.

How can I change that? I remembered how someone had told me about a "blessings list." *Another list? This is getting ridiculous.* But I knew it could help so I started writing. Ten minutes later, I was surprised at how many blessings I had thought of. My heart felt bubbly with thanksgiving.

After I put that list on the refrigerator next to the others, I picked up the book again. *Almost done.*

Finally I came to the last step: "Repeat the above formula each time you are angry." I laughed out loud. *Okay, God, I understand the point. This isn't going to be a one-time thing but a process. I don't particularly like the idea. I thought you would want me to have an instantaneous deliverance so you could be glorified. But since you haven't answered "yes," I guess you have a different plan. It sure doesn't make sense to me. Help me to trust you know what you're doing because my way is only eating my heart out and destroying my family.*

Now that I know the seven steps, how can I be reminded to follow them, Lord? Another list on the refrigerator? I laughed out loud. But I knew it wasn't funny. I often said I was going to try something and then forgot all about it. Since there wasn't any more room on the refrigerator, I copied the seven steps down on a card and taped it to the window above my kitchen sink. *I'm going to memorize them and be reminded to use them. I think I spend more time at the kitchen sink than almost anywhere else, anyway.*

I found a large, lined card in the junk drawer in the kitchen and wrote the steps down. *Lord, please help me follow them. And help me get back to disciplining Darcy consistently. That helped me so much before. Maybe if I'm faithful to both of these projects, I really will see victory. Jesus, I've got to. I don't know how much longer I can go on like this without doing something horribly bad. I'll depend on you to remind me often.*

At that moment, it felt like the Holy Spirit told me what to do: "Put verses about anger throughout the house."

That's a good idea, Lord. I fished out more cards, wrote out verses referring to anger and taped them in prominent places in the rooms I went into most often. Now when I washed the dishes or fixed meals, I read the seven steps again and again until I had memorized them.

When I led Darcy into the bathroom after a potty training accident, I studied the card on the mirror which included Ephesians 4:31-32. "Let all bitterness and wrath and anger and clamor and slander be put away from you, along with all malice. Be kind to one another, tenderhearted, forgiving one another, as God in Christ forgave you."

On my bathroom mirror, the card with Proverbs 10:12 reminded me how to love Darcy: "Hatred stirs up strife, but love covers all offenses." I memorized it and repeated it to myself. It reminded me my anger only made things worse, not better. Why would I choose it?

In Darcy's room, I put Proverbs 15:18: "A hot-tempered man stirs up strife, but he who is slow to anger quiets contention."

As the next few weeks went along, I went through the steps over and over again and it seemed like I wasn't reacting with anger as often. And if I did, it wasn't explosive. The light at the end of the train tunnel was growing. Maybe God loved me and my family after all.

God's love also appeared in an unexpected way in my attitude toward Larry. Since I'd obeyed his command of thinking "I love you," it seemed easier to repeat the phrase. I hadn't said the words out loud but when the seven steps encouraged me to forgive others, I applied it more often to Larry. My heart seemed to see him with new eyes. *Maybe he isn't capable of giving the love I need. Is he even supposed to, Lord?*

Don't think that way. Don't think that way, reverberated through my heart. *He is responsible. Don't believe the lie. Why else should I be married?* The thought of not holding him responsible terrified me. But almost without my permission, the thick wall of hate toward him was thinning. I couldn't help but more often notice the little things he did to love on Darcy. When she laughed in delight in response, it didn't grate on my nerves as much. And I'd never noticed how often he gathered Mark into his lap and handed him a rattle.

But it's not enough. It's not enough argued in return. But each time I followed God's prompting to think "I love you," the choice was easier to make.

Then I began attending a class for women at church. Our teacher seemed to know the condition of my heart. Her theme encouraged us to choose joy. The Holy Spirit seemed to bring her words uninvited into my mind, molding them to address my wall of bitterness. "Wonder if he never changes, are you going to be unhappy for the rest of your life?" and "Why put your happiness into the hands of another?" "He doesn't have to ruin you. It's your choice whether you have joy." God seemed to be beckoning, "I can give you the joy you need. Happiness is something happening to you but joy is something you receive from me."

These new ideas unsettled me but the more often I allowed them to pull down the bricks shoring up the wall of protection, the more they seemed true. I wasn't sure I liked the softening of my heart. When would the rejection come again?

One day as the truths melted my resolve and before I could replace the bricks, I agreed to the prompting in my heart. I solemnly readied a pail of soapy water with a sponge as if in preparation for a consecrated ceremony. I went into the laundry room and washed off the rotting apple pieces off the ceiling and walls.

"God, I no longer need a memorial to my rotten marriage. I choose to trust you for whatever happens. Even if Larry never changes, you can provide for my needs beyond his abilities. He may never be able to be what I need, but you can be. I'm going to continue thinking those three words of love. Please bring me to the place I can actually say them out loud and believe them. And in the meantime, I forgive and release Larry from being responsible for my happiness. I'm going to stop nagging him and trying to manipulate him with anger. He's yours for the changes you want."

By the time the ceiling and wall were clean, I was sobbing in surrender on my knees.

"Mommy, Mommy, what's wrong? You okay?" Darcy put her hand on my shoulder as if she were trying to lift me up.

"It's okay, honey. Mommy is fine." I hugged her tight. "Mommy is more than fine. Mommy is being set free."

CHAPTER 16

VICTORY IN SIGHT

August 30

My blurry mind struggled to wake up as my eyes focused on the clock: 8:04. Snapping alert, I listened for the children but didn't hear a sound. Evidently, Darcy and Mark weren't awake yet. I was surprised. Remembering today was the mom's church group, I had to hurry.

As I dressed, I heard Darcy playing in her room and Mark babbling in his crib. Even though I started to feel rushed, I was happy. The past two weeks had gone smoothly. By repeating the seven steps, I had been able to catch myself almost every time my anger had started to erupt.

Darcy ran into my bedroom. "Mommy, what we having for breakfast?"

"Oatmeal and toast," I replied, putting on my sandals.

"I want pancakes. Pancakes, please, Mommy."

"No, Darcy, we had pancakes yesterday. I don't want you to have too much syrup."

Darcy's face puckered up into a tearless cry.

Rushing past her into Mark's room, I began dressing him. I heard Darcy screaming in my bedroom: my chest and throat tightened. *Oh, Lord, I don't need her to have a temper tantrum when we're in a hurry. But step number five says to give thanks for anything that bothers me, so thank you, Lord, that Darcy is having a fit.* I smiled. *This is almost comical. Here I am changing Mark's dirty diaper and being grateful Darcy is screaming in the next room.*

Mark lay on his back on the changing table sucking his fist. His round, chubby belly wiggled as I wiped off his bottom. The phone rang. I picked up Mark's naked body and raced to answer it. It was Claudia asking for a ride to the meeting. I assured her I could be at her house at 9:15. When she continued to talk, I sighed helplessly. How could I tactfully get her to hang up? But within a few minutes she finished. I hung up the phone and noticed it was 8:30.

By the time we ate breakfast and I dressed Darcy, it was 9:00. I hadn't even packed Mark's diaper bag yet. My tension increased as Darcy asked question after question, and to make things worse I couldn't find my keys.

When I had finally packed the bag and found my keys, I was perspiring and gritting my teeth. I strapped Mark into his car seat and reached for Darcy. I felt something wet. *Oh, no, it can't be. Not now, when we're late.*

"Darcy, are your pants wet?" Her frightened face stared up at me. "You've been doing so well. Why did you pick this morning to have an accident?"

I gripped her arm tightly and pulled her into the house. Her little legs struggled to keep up. "Honest to God, Darcy, why now? Are you doing this on purpose?"

My tension turned to fury. "Now we'll be late and Claudia is waiting for us. What will she think of me, certainly not I'm very dependable." I continued to spew out my frustration.

As I grappled to pull down Darcy's clinging training pants, I noticed the verse on the mirror. "Let all bitterness and wrath ..." I don't care about that. She's doing this on purpose. She's got to be. She's been doing so well the last couple of weeks.

I was jumping up and down inside. *I'm going be late ... Claudia is waiting ... She's going to think I'm not dependable.*

I jerked my hand back and let it slam against Darcy's wet bottom.

"Next time you better tell me first," I yelled. By the time I had hit Darcy five times, shame replaced my anger.

I escaped into Darcy's room searching for another pair of training pants. Returning to the bathroom, guilt and failure overwhelmed me. "See, Darcy, that's what happens when you wet your pants," I defended myself. But inside, I cried out, "Oh no, I've done it again. I can't believe it. I've been doing so well and now I've blown it."

I picked up Darcy and carried her out to the car. Tears tumbled down my face as I drove the car out of the garage. *Dear Jesus, I'm so ashamed. When am I ever going to learn? When am I ever going to get complete control? Do I have to practice the seven steps again?*

At first, I didn't want to go through them. Then I remembered how much I had learned in the last couple of weeks. If I ignored my outbursts, I didn't have the Holy Spirit's power to resist becoming angry the next time. But when I followed the seven steps, I sensed a renewing, cleansing power enabling me to control myself during the next aggravating situation.

All right, Lord, here I go again. Father, I confess my outburst and spanking Darcy in anger as sin. I ask you to forgive me and to cleanse me even though I don't deserve it. I believe 1 John 1:9 is true: when I confess, you forgive and cleanse.

I turned to Darcy and couldn't look into her eyes. "Darcy, will you forgive me for getting angry with you?"

Darcy's tear-stained face gazed at me uncomprehendingly. I knew she didn't know what forgive meant but I needed to ask for her forgiveness anyway. Many times in the past weeks, I had consciously not become angry so I wouldn't have to ask for her forgiveness.

Focusing on the Lord again, I muttered, "Jesus, I forgive Darcy for having an accident. Help me to remember she doesn't do it on purpose, she's still learning. Thank you, Darcy's accidents are helping me control my anger habit because then I depend upon your strength and not my own. It seems like it's taking a long time but I know I'm in the process of learning, too."

I looked into the rearview mirror to wipe my face. Then I reached back and wiped off Darcy's face. We pulled into Claudia's driveway and she got into the car with her three-year-old daughter. Hoping I didn't look too upset, I apologized for being late but Claudia only said it didn't matter. She quickly shared her excitement over her daughter's latest accomplishment.

When we arrived at the park, I hurriedly set out the blanket and placed Mark beside me. Gathering Darcy into my lap, Amanda started the meeting with prayer. As a regular part of the meeting, everyone shared stories about their month and this time most of the women expressed how much they loved being moms.

Guilt plundered my heart of peace and joy. It screamed within me, "What a terrible mother you are. You beat your kid and nobody else does."

No, no. God has forgiven me. He's forgotten about it and I'm cleansed.

"How can you call yourself a Christian the way you act?"
I'm not perfect, but Jesus is my Savior.

When it was my turn to share, I mumbled something about how Mark was tasting more foods. But all the while I wondered, *Don't any of them get angry sometimes? Will I ever have complete victory? Does God still love me even though I've failed him? Why don't I experience the joys of motherhood like everyone else? No one else talks about getting angry.*

After everyone had shared, Darcy played with the other children at the playground a few feet away while I tried to look cheerful visiting with my friends. It was close to lunchtime when I dropped Claudia off at her house. Darcy whined complaints about being hungry, but I tried to tune them out.

Think positive. Think positive. I began singing "Jesus Loves Me" and Darcy joined in. With a sigh of relief, I drove into our garage, unloaded everyone and everything into the house, and quickly fixed peanut and jelly sandwiches.

As I handed Darcy her sandwich, guilt sent a barrage of bullets and my heart surrendered. *I'm the worst there is.* Guilt then raised a victory flag. Refilling my truth gun, I shot back, *I failed but at least I'm not failing as often. Most of the time I'm able to catch myself before I'm out of control. I guess it's just going to take more time.*

In the next month, I coped with stressful situations better than I ever had before. When Mark came down with another cold and was coughing through the nights, I napped every afternoon, and regularly reviewed the seven steps.

Then I came down with Mark's cold. Although my body was weak and easily irritated, I monitored my thoughts carefully to prevent negative thinking from capturing my mind.

I continued to discipline Darcy consistently and eventually her misbehavior was slightly reduced. Her third birthday was coming soon, so I hoped she was growing out of the "terrible twos."

Little by little, like grains of sand dropping through an hourglass, I was seeing victory mount up in a pile. God was working, and for the first time I confidently knew someday I was going to be in control of my anger. Now when people complimented me on my patience with Darcy in public, I could smile and say "thank you" instead of mentally rejecting their praise. Maybe I wasn't such a bad mother after all.

CHAPTER 17

LOVED

September 15

Picking up the phone, I heard a woman's voice say, "Kathy Miller, please."

"That's me."

"Kathy, this is Joy from Christian Women's Club. We've noticed how regularly you come to the monthly luncheons and wonder whether you'd consider serving as Nursery Chair on our new board beginning in October. We'd really love to have you serve the Lord with us."

"Oh, my. What would the position entail?"

"It means you would attend the luncheons to collect the money for the babysitters, and also come to the two other board meetings we have each month."

"Oh, I see." I was flattered they wanted me to join their board but I knew I couldn't agree to such a commitment with all the other things I had to do. *I know what Larry will say if I take on another responsibility.*

"Well," I answered, "I'm really glad you thought of me. But ... uh, I really don't think I could at this time. My son is only nine months old and is still nursing. It's hard for me to leave him for very long. So I don't think I could. But I really do appreciate you asking me. I enjoy the luncheons so much and you women certainly do a great job of putting it together."

Joy's disappointed voice replied, "I'm sorry it won't work out now, but do keep us in mind for the future, ok?"

We said goodbye.

I smiled as I thought about Joy's offer. It would be exciting to be involved in something bringing women closer to Christ. But I really did have too much to do already and it would be hard on Mark to leave him so often. Even though he was eating more solid foods, he was not ready to wean yet. He'd never wanted to take a bottle, even if it was breast milk. The peace in my heart confirmed my decision.

But within a few days, the thought of joining the board resurfaced in my mind. *Wow, that really would be fabulous to be involved. I'd love to get to know those gals. They could really encourage me and I need it. Well, that's just the problem, Kathy, you're not mature enough to be ministering to others. Forget it. Your life is a mess. You disappoint God a lot with your disobedience.*

It was easy to bury the idea in the "not now, maybe next year" cubbyhole of my mind as I thought about the responsibilities of my family, Bible study, and maintaining my patience. I didn't need any new pressures to undermine my control. I was sailing along better and better, seldom losing control, I didn't want anything to complicate my life.

Even though I continued to bury the thought, it kept digging itself out of the hole. *Besides, it's too late now, they must have found someone else.*

A week later, as I visited with my sister, Karen, another woman from the club called. "Kathy, we on the nominating committee were wondering if by any chance you'd thought any more about joining us as Nursery Chair. The Lord hasn't filled that position yet. We're wondering if he's keeping it open for you."

Unable to restrain myself, I giggled. "Well, as a matter of fact, I have been thinking about it but I assumed the position would be filled already. I don't know what to say. Can I call you back after I've prayed and also talked to my husband?"

She agreed and gave me her number.

My heart raced with joy as I hung up the phone and explained to Karen what had happened. She laughed. "It sure looks like the Lord wants you to join the board, doesn't it?"

"Boy, it sure does. But I don't know what Larry will say. He always says I have enough to do. And this position seems to require more time and responsibility than I've usually tackled. And what about Mark? How can I leave him for the extra meetings which are so much longer than the luncheons?"

"Well," Karen smiled, "if the Lord wants you to do it, he'll show you the way."

The rest of the day I felt excited, yet a little apprehensive, about talking with Larry. How could I ask him in such a way he might say yes? *Lord, if it's your will, you're going to have to work with me on this one.*

The next morning after Larry finished breakfast, I sat at the table with him. I explained how both Joy and Virginia had called and asked me to be on the board, and how I had increasingly sensed the Lord changing my desires.

Taking a deep breath, I asked, "Honey, what do you think about me joining the board as Nursery Chair?"

He stared at the hanging tiffany-styled lamp above us. Barely breathing, I waited and prayed, *Lord, guide him according to your will. But I really want to join the board … please.*

He turned to me. "You really think this is what the Lord wants you to do?"

I was a little surprised by his amiableness and how it seemed right to say, "Yes, I do."

"Then it seems fine with me."

Bursting with joy, I clapped my hands. *Thank you, Jesus, thank you. You want me to do it.*

"Larry," I grinned and kissed him, "I'm thrilled you said that. I'm so excited."

I immediately reached for the phone on the wall. My hand shook as I dialed Virginia's number, and the happiness she expressed after hearing my answer was reassuring.

I eagerly looked forward to the first board meeting on October fifth—only two weeks away—when the new officers would be introduced.

The next week, Mark suddenly started to balk at nursing. I couldn't imagine why he wouldn't want to nurse. His gums were bothering him a little from teething, but I didn't think that would prevent him from nursing altogether. He was becoming a lot more interested in food and he loved drinking from a cup, but I had expected him to nurse longer.

He's close to ten months old. Darcy nursed till she was fifteen months. This seems so strange. There doesn't seem to be anything wrong happening though. He's eating solid food well.

The morning of the board meeting, I stood at the sink washing the breakfast dishes when an awareness of God's guidance and work broke through to my soul like the sun bursting through the clouds after a storm.

Why, of course, this will help me leave him in the nursery longer for the luncheons and the extra meetings. Oh, Lord, your perfect timing. Thank you for this confirmation.

You are doing all this for me, aren't you? I can't believe it. You're showing me over and over again you are specifically leading me. Your hand is upon me. Even though I've abused Darcy and I'm not in complete control, yet, you still love me. I'm important to you and you haven't given up on me.

Tears brimmed in my eyes, then plopped into the sudsy dishwater below my bowed face. The realization of God's love for me was overwhelming. "God loves me ... again!" I cried out loud, hesitantly mouthing the word "again."

He had never stopped loving me, but the light of the fact had been dissipated in my heart by anger and depression. But now it's full strength dispersed all the gloom.

I love you, Lord. I love you so very much. Astonished, I paused in thought. *I haven't told God I love him for so long. It's been such a long time since I've felt loved by him and felt loving toward him. But now I want to shout it from the rooftops. God has shown me how much he loves me and I love him, too. He wants me to serve him; he wants to guide me; he wants me to receive his love and hope.*

I couldn't wipe the joyous smile off my face for a week--and I didn't want to. Darcy's temper tantrums didn't bother me. *God loves me.* Mark's teething fussiness didn't faze me. *God cares for me.* The messy house didn't overwhelm me. *God is guiding me.*

Larry couldn't believe the change he saw in me. When he asked why I was so happy, I replied, "Honey, God loves me. He's shown me how much he loves me. Can you believe it?"

Larry's quizzical look didn't dilute my joy. "But I thought you knew he loved you."

"Yes, but I had lost the joy of his love, of realizing he specifically loves and cares about my life. He has guided me to join the board. Everything happening—you allowing me to join the board, Mark suddenly weaning himself—it all points to God moving in my life. I'm important to him."

Larry laughed. "Well, I'm glad it's meant so much to you. That's great."

He started to turn back to reading the newspaper when he paused and leaned toward me. "And you know I love you too, right?"

I had to swallow back my shock. It had been so long since he'd said words like that. What was going on?

Larry unexpectedly continued. "You've seemed different for more than a month. Even before this board thing came up. It doesn't seem like you're as desperately needy for me to come through for you. I have to admit it's been nice. Thank you. In fact, I was thinking we've got to find some time to get together." Larry winked as he nodded his head toward Darcy as if to protect her from hearing intimate words. "Tomorrow afternoon when the kids are down for their naps, wake me up and join me, okay?"

I swallowed again. "And I love you too. That would be great. Okay, I will."

Larry put down the newspaper, gave me a lingering kiss with his hands cupping my face, and left the room. I wanted to drop to my knees in worship, but it might look really awkward if he came back into the room. Instead, I bowed my head and whispered, "Oh, Lord. I said the three words out loud. I can't believe it. It wasn't completely natural, but I said them. Not just because Larry is reaching out to me but because you are softening my heart. Thank you. Thank you. You're meeting my needs and now Larry notices. I didn't think it would happen, but it is. Oh, you are so clever. It started out with a thought and ended in reality. Oh, yes, you are indeed clever."

Since I'd made that decision to love Larry—even though I'd only thought it and not said it, it had been easier to believe it could be true. I'd even begun to notice his positive responses I would have cast away in the past. God really was changing my heart and now I could tell Larry I loved him. Even if he had rejected me or said something demeaning, it wouldn't have mattered. My feelings about myself were less and less dependent upon his reactions.

The light coming toward me in the tunnel was ever brighter. God could be trusted to provide for my needs. And one of my needs to have fellowship with other Christian women in ministry had come true. My heart swelled with love and gratitude. *Thank you, God. Larry doesn't have to provide for all my needs. You can.*

CHAPTER 18

NOT PERFECT YET

October 15

Three years old. I can't believe it. Darcy turned three on October twelfth. I smiled at her sitting on the floor watching Sesame Street. *Oh, Father, thank you for this last month. It has been glorious. I've rarely been out of control, but more importantly, I love you and know you love me. Well, at least, most of the time. And I know now I'll never go back to my old anger habit.*

I stared again at my to-do list for the family birthday party for Darcy in the evening. I was so glad Larry would be off work to help me. As soon as he returned from his real estate appointment he could set up the tables and chairs and stay with the kids while I did some last minute shopping. He'd said he wouldn't be gone long. I figured he should be home around one o'clock.

"Oh, wait, did I tell him I needed him to come right home so he could help me?" I couldn't remember exactly saying it but certainly he would know I needed his help.

The newfound loving connection growing between us had also been glorious. It wasn't all I hoped for, but it was obvious God was working in this area too. I could freely tell him I loved him and he began telling me again also.

As I stirred the cake mix, I glanced at the clock. "Okay, Darcy, it's ten o'clock; time to turn off the television. That's enough cartoons for this morning."

"Longer, Mommy, please, longer." Darcy frowned and a small tremor of terror erupted inside me. *Not another temper tantrum! They make me feel so defeated.*

Well, she is the birthday girl so maybe she can. Oh, wait, when I've let her watch TV longer in the past, it's been twice as hard to get her to turn it off the next day. No, it'll be better if I remain firm on my rule. Following through with consequences for disobedience has really made a difference. Thank you, Lord.

"No, sweetheart. Besides, we're getting ready for your birthday party, remember? Go play with your new toys you received at the kids' party the other day. Your new dolly will be lots of fun to play with."

Pouting, Darcy turned off the television with a flourish of her hand. *She will make a good actress someday.*

After she skipped down the hall toward her bedroom, I turned away and headed for the kitchen to grab a cake pan. After putting it in the oven, I retrieved the vacuum cleaner out of the hall closet. I wished I had done more things the day before, but my battle with the flu had made me unmotivated.

Heading back down the hall, Mark crawled past me toward his yarn ball. "Hey, Mark, you're really going to town with your crawling, aren't you?" Reaching down, I picked up the soft, multicolored yarn ball and tossed it out in front of him. With a squeal, he crawled toward it.

The phone rang. It was my sister asking for some ideas for a birthday gift for Darcy. Then we started talking about other things and before I knew it, twenty minutes had passed.

Hanging up the phone, I dashed down the hall, looking in each room for Darcy and Mark. I looked over into the family room and saw Darcy--still in front of the television. *How did I not hear her turn that back on?* Mark sat nearby trying to put the plastic circles over the tower. I pushed the off button on the TV. Startled, Darcy looked up and started to cry.

"Darcy, I told you. No more television." I wanted to yell but I lowered my voice.

Darcy began pounding the floor with her fists.

When are these temper tantrums going to stop? I thought she was over the terrible twos now. At least there has been a slight improvement.

I turned on my heels and grabbed the vacuum, quickly plugging it in. I began vacuuming in the living room as I gritted my teeth. In the adjacent family room, I could see Darcy continuing to pound her fists on the floor. Icy chills traveled down my back and my chest muscles tensed.

She's got to learn. As I thought of everything I still needed to do, anger erupted within me. I envisioned me jerking her up by her arm and giving her a hard swat. My voice rose as I exclaimed, "Darcy, we're going to stop this right now." My long strides placed me within eyesight of the kitchen and my eyes settled on my lists on the refrigerator. I stopped and took a deep breath, exhaling slowly.

All right, Kathy, calm down. Yes, Darcy disobeyed but she's only a little girl. You're not perfect yet and neither is she. Your anger is not going to make her obey. Remember Proverbs 15:1? "A soft answer turns away wrath, but a harsh word stirs up anger." Anger only enflames the situation. It doesn't accomplish what you want. And it's not a disciplinary tool. Only consequences help.

I continued to breathe deeply. I felt calmer as I made a detour into the kitchen to get the wooden spoon to spank her. It had become a good friend because I took the time to retrieve it and to calm down. I couldn't just haul off and smack Darcy.

I reached Darcy and when she saw the spoon, her mouth dropped open. "No more TV, Mommy. I promise. No spanking, please?"

"Yes, Darcy, I do have to spank you so you'll remember next time not to turn on the television without permission."

After swatting Darcy three times on her bottom firmly but without anger, I cuddled her as we talked about why it was important for her to obey me. Then I diverted the conversation to her birthday party and her face brightened at the prospects of cake and gifts.

"Darcy, Mommy really needs your help, OK? I'm making your birthday special. I have a lot to do. Can you play nicely while I dust, and then it will be time for lunch, okay?"

She nodded and jumped off my lap running into her room. I heard her fishing several toys out of her overflowing toy box.

Feeling relieved, I put Mark in his playpen and dusted the living room furniture. As I thought about all the other projects I had wanted to accomplish, I grimaced. Tension began constricting my chest. I reminded myself, "It's okay to settle for whatever I can do. I can give up my perfectionistic expectations. No one will care or even know what isn't done."

I reminded myself about the perfectionistic tendencies I was discovering within me. I had been recognizing my "all or nothing" attitudes like if everything wasn't done, I couldn't be satisfied. Now I was learning to be content with whatever I could accomplish. It was just as pleasing and less stressful.

Sighing in resignation, I finished dusting and then fixed lunch. We finished lunch and surprisingly, both Darcy and Mark fell asleep easily. It was already 1:30 and the clock raced faster. *Larry still isn't home. Where is he? Lord, please prompt him to come home soon. I really need him.*

Sitting near the front window, I expected to see Larry's car drive up any moment. I decided to read a magazine. *No use getting started on a big project since I will be interrupted.* After thirty minutes, I decided I needed to get back to work, even if Larry wasn't home.

As I took my china out of the cupboard, I found myself fuming. *Why is he late? He must know we have a lot to do to get ready for the party. Anyone would know that. I can't set up the heavy table all by myself. Where is he?*

My anticipation evolved into greater anger during the next hour. Realizing stress was choking out my trust in the Lord's timing, I paused to quote some verses on anger. I sensed temporary relief and thanked the Lord. But when Larry still didn't arrive, the tension returned.

Father, please make him come home soon. There is too much for me to do alone. And please help me with this anger I feel. I've really been trying to control my emotions. And I don't want to make Larry feel guilty when he comes home. Right now, I submit to your plan and timetable for today. I thank you that you are in control and I can trust you. Everything you want done will get done.

I felt peace wash away my anger and tension. It was exciting to see the Lord helping me again. It seemed his immediate peace was always available as soon as I relaxed in his control. I had experienced it happening over and over again.

Suddenly, I heard the sound of the garage door moving and the hum of the car. "Lord, thank you. You're helping me to have the right attitude."

Larry rushed into the bedroom where I was folding clothes. "Hey, honey, I'm sorry I'm late but I went by Bob's for a while. He's still pretty sick even though he's doing a bit better. He might be able to get back to work in about a month."

I expected my anger to flare but instead, I sensed the peace within as strongly as I had felt it earlier. *Thank you, Lord, you are teaching me to relax in you.*

"I'm so glad he's doing better. That was thoughtful of you to visit him."

"I've been meaning to get over to see him for a long time and decided I better do it today and stop putting it off."

Setting his keys down on top of the bureau, he turned to face me. His dark hair and hazel eyes appeared especially handsome. He grasped my hands and pulled me down with him onto the bed. "You know what? I sure do appreciate you. I'm glad you're not sick." He wrapped his arms around me.

I tried to pout but giggled instead. "You do, huh? I don't know if I appreciate you. I wanted you to come right home so you could help me get everything ready for the birthday party tonight."

Larry began to pull away but I held his arms around me.

"It's my fault, don't worry," I interjected. "I forgot to tell you. I thought you would realize it. Don't get me wrong. Now I'm glad you went to see Bob, but I sure was getting angry with you when you were late."

"Honey, I can't read your mind. You've got to tell me otherwise I don't know. Of course I'll help you." He started to sit up but I pushed him back down.

"Larry," I paused, clarifying my thoughts. "I realize I do expect you to be a mind reader. I'm always thinking you should automatically know my needs and then meet them. I'm going to try to remember to share things with you more."

"So start now." Larry gazed intently into my eyes.

I diverted my eyes from his and smoothed back his hair from his forehead. "Well, I guess one of my needs these days is for more attention. Unfortunately, when I've tried to tell you in the past, I haven't been able to do it without creating misunderstanding for you being gone."

I stared into his eyes. "So, let me change my appeal a little by requesting we talk more when you're home. Maybe somehow, we can have more time to communicate and air our feelings. Sometimes I feel so alone. With everyone else's husband home in the evenings, I really start to feel cheated."

"Kathy, I can understand your feeling. From now on we'll try to talk more. Maybe we won't turn on the television so soon after the kids have gone to bed. How does that sound?"

"That would be fantastic!" I leaned over and kissed him.

I jumped up from the bed laughing. "And now I request we get ready for Darcy's third birthday party. Let's go."

Larry replied, "Ok, will do, captain." He saluted with a playful grin.

Grabbing his arm, I pulled him up in mock strength. After I told him what things needed to be done, I left to finish my shopping.

Falling into bed after everyone was gone and the kids tucked into bed I reflected on the great time Darcy had at her birthday party. Everything wasn't perfect like I intended, but Darcy didn't notice and neither did anyone else. But more important to me was my calm and peaceful attitude. I wasn't perfect yet, but God was empowering me to handle my anger well more often. I was content and on my way to victory.

CHAPTER 19

FORGIVEN

November 15

Mom and I relaxed on my living room couch planning Thanksgiving dinner, only a week away. Darcy handed me her doll to dress and then brought a game to play.

My mother laughed. "Well, Kathy, you might as well find something we can all do together. Darcy doesn't want to be left out."

"Yeah, I guess you're right. At least it's not too long until her bedtime. Darcy, would you like us to play ball with you?" I knew we could talk even as we rolled a ball back and forth. "Grandma and I will roll the ball on the carpet and you can jump over it, okay?"

Darcy's eyes brightened in delight and she quickly retrieved her red plastic ball from her room.

"Ready." She stood anticipating the first pass of the ball with a huge grin on her face.

I positioned myself on the carpet, a few feet away from my mother. We rolled the ball back and forth while continuing to plan the dinner. Each time the ball rolled across, Darcy took careful aim and jumped over it with a squeal of joy.

"Now, what will we serve for dessert?" my mom asked.

"Of course, pumpkin pie and ..." Then I gasped in horror as Darcy jumped on top of the ball. Her feet flew out from beneath her and with a sickening thud, the back of her head slammed down onto the carpet.

I froze as Mom reached over and cradled Darcy's rigid body in her arms. A moment later, Darcy's body fell limp and her head dangled over my mom's arm. My mother started gently wiggling Darcy's face, calling, "Darcy, Darcy, wake up."

"Oh, no, Mom. She's unconscious," I yelled and jumped to my feet. "I'm going to call the paramedics." I ran to the phone in the family room and picked up the receiver with trembling hands.

My mom shouted, "She's conscious again."

I put the receiver back and ran to gather Darcy into my arms. Darcy's eyes were open but she looked dazed. I cupped her face in my hands. "Honey, how do you feel?"

Her eyes tried to focus on me and her head wobbled in my hands. "My head hurts." She lifted her hand to touch her head.

"Okay, honey. It's bound to hurt considering how hard you hit." I lifted her and sat on the couch.

Mom and I sat there for a while discussing what we should do. Soon, Darcy complained, "Mommy, tummy feel sick. I want to go to sleep."

I tried to smile but my lips felt heavy. "That's the first time in her whole life she's volunteered to go to sleep." But I knew it wasn't funny. It was a sign of concussion.

Lifting Darcy into my mother's lap, I said, "I'm going to call our clinic and see what they say." The nurse said to take her to the nearest emergency room; we arrived ten minutes later. My mom stayed with Mark at home and promised she would call Larry at work to tell him to meet me.

I carried sleeping Darcy through the emergency room doors which softly whisked open as I approached and then closed behind me. I explained what happened to the woman sitting behind a counter. After quickly filling out paperwork as I cradled Darcy in my lap, the nurse escorted us to a bed surrounded by white curtains. The antiseptic smells made my stomach queasy.

Dr. Monning walked into our cubicle and introduced himself. He asked me several questions and then explained they would take a skull x-ray. A few minutes later, with Darcy laying on the bed, a technician arrived and wheeled her away.

It seemed like hours later when they returned. Darcy was still asleep and looked so little in the big bed. Her peaceful face appeared angelic and innocent.

"Oh, Darcy," I murmured, "I hope you're going to be all right." I caught myself. "No, that's not true. I don't want you to be all right. I wonder if I would really be that sad if you died. Sometimes I think I hate you. I long to be freed of the responsibilities and burdens of being a mother." I stopped. *I'm not supposed to feel this way, what a horrible mother I am.* But I knew I couldn't hold the feelings in any longer. I let my thoughts continue.

I wanted a child so much, Darcy. We tried for three years before you were conceived, and now I wonder whether I want you around at all. You demand so much from me. Sometimes I want to be free.

I felt ashamed, but at the same time, it felt like a heavy burden was being lifted off my heart. I was finally being honest with myself. Tears welled in my eyes.

Darcy, I haven't hurt you for a long time and I'm not going to again … but I still resent you. You seem to want more from me than I am able to give. I'm trying to trust God for the future but I wonder if I've hurt you permanently, psychologically. I read somewhere children who have been abused usually grow up to abuse their own children.

I whispered, "Oh, Heavenly Father, I don't want that to happen. Please protect Darcy. Please keep her safe from such a future. You know I never wanted to hurt her. You know I'm sorry. Please forgive me and heal Darcy's inner wounds." God's forgiveness seemed to cleanse my heart.

I stared at my little girl. Pulling a tissue out of my purse, I wiped my cheeks and blew my nose.

"Kathy, how is she doing?"

Larry's voice startled me. I stood up and reached for him to give me a hug. "The doctor hasn't said anything yet. They just took an x-ray. I'm so glad you're here."

As I shared with Larry the details of what had happened, Dr. Monning walked in and the men shook hands. Then the doctor explained, "Mr. and Mrs. Miller, Darcy does have a concussion but she'll be fine. There's no damage. You can take her home. Just keep an eye on her extra close for twenty-four hours. Wake her up through the night every four hours or so. Call your doctor if you notice anything wrong."

The next day, Darcy played as hard as ever. I watched her and was particularly aware of her bright smile and loving vivaciousness. I thought of how much I would have missed these moments if anything had happened to her. The realization became stronger as the day progressed and I felt a stirring of love in my heart for her. Yes, I would have missed her if she were gone. *Thank you, Lord, for our delightful daughter who brings joy into our family. I do love her. I do want her here with us.*

That night as I tucked her into bed, I stroked her bangs back from her forehead. Love overwhelmed me and I wanted to cry in relief.

Darcy, I do love you. I didn't think I did, but the Lord has shown me how much I really do. It still hurts me to think of how I used to hurt you, but I'm going to trust the Lord to heal all of us. In the meantime, I know he has forgiven me.

"Mommy, tickle my back." Darcy loved to have her back tickled and usually it made me feel so frustrated and trapped. I just wanted to go do what I thought I needed to do. But this time, I was glad to love her this way.

When I could tell she was about to fall asleep, I leaned over and kissed her forehead. I whispered, "Good night, Dars. Sleep tight." I walked to the door and turned off the light.

"Mommy, I love you," Darcy's sleepy voice called out.

I turned to face her in the dark. "Oh, Darcy, I love you very much." I was so glad I could say and mean it. "Good night, honey. You are God's special gift."

CHAPTER 20

IN CONTROL

December 3

November stepped aside to make room for a festive December. It was hard to believe it was Mark's first birthday. Where had the year gone? It was a bitter sweet year that in some ways I never wanted but in other ways, I saw God's work. It was hard to put the two together, but I decided I didn't have to figure it out. It was all right if I never did.

With the preparations for Christmas it was easier to divert my attention. Christmas decorations draped the streets and almost every television commercial advertised some new toy or gift. Darcy grew more excited each day thinking all the toys, dolls, and miscellaneous trinkets advertised on television were going to be hers.

November had meant celebrating Thanksgiving. But for me every day was a thanksgiving, a giving of thanks and praise to the Lord who was delivering me from my anger.

At the December Christian Women's Club board meeting, Joy announced plans for the board's Christmas party. It was to be a formal evening for couples and sounded exciting. But when she informed us it would be on Tuesday night, December twentieth, disappointment filled my heart. Larry worked on Tuesday nights.

When I mentioned the party to him the next day, his saddened face disclosed it would be impossible for him to take the night off. But somehow, an unexpected peace grew within my heart as I calmly told him, "Sweetheart, I'm sure if the Lord wants you to go with me, he'll somehow find a way for it to happen."

Larry's skeptical frown almost pricked my ballooning hope, but I reminded myself of Proverbs 3:5-6 which I had been trying to keep at the center of my thoughts for the last week. "Trust in the Lord with all your heart, and do not lean on your own understanding. In all your ways acknowledge him, and he will make straight your paths." Even if it meant going to the party by myself, I was determined to trust the Lord and not get uptight.

As Christmas drew closer, Mark became increasingly fussy with teething. Just when he had started sleeping consistently through the night, I was once again being awakened by his pained cries.

One Wednesday around midnight, Mark's squall invaded my dream. In a fogged haze of weariness, I pushed myself up out of bed and made my way to his room.

Picking him up out of his crib, I soothed, "Oh, Mark, are your teeth hurting again? You are really having a hard time with them aren't you? Let's go get some aspirin."

After giving him the medicine, I laid him on my shoulder and sleepily sank down into the rocking chair. As it squeaked softly amidst the silent, cool night air, I prayed, *Dear Lord, help Mark's gums stop hurting now so we can get back to sleep.*

The placidity enveloped me and my mind and heart absorbed the loveliness of the moment. Even though my body yearned for the warmth of my bed, my spirit longed to praise the Lord.

Oh, Father, you are doing such marvelous things in my life. I stand in awe at your power ... and your forgiveness. Lord, you've forgiven me so many times and yet I know you'll have to forgive me many more times for so many things. I smiled. *But at least not as often as before about my anger.*

I still experienced eruptions of anger and frustration, but it wasn't unbridled anger any longer. I was in control through God's power. Life was beautiful and Jesus never seemed so real. My devotions took on a new luster like the sparkling Christmas ornaments around me. I loved working on the Christian Women's Club board. The Lord used me there and I had a purpose for living.

I was loved and that love was flowing onto Darcy. I still battled anger, frustration, and stress, but instead of believing I was losing the battle, I knew I had won the war. Victory was mine. Life was challenging but exciting.

Lord, my marriage isn't exactly the way I want it to be, but I give you the credit for what's happening. Of course, I want it better. There's no guarantee Larry will become the godly man I long for, but I'll trust you for whatever happens. Right now, I'm content to continue accepting Larry as he is and to work on my greater patience and joy.

The impact of my reverie cascaded onto my soul like a waterfall streaming down rocks into a clear, sparkling pool. My heart burst with thanksgiving and joy. "Lord, you have delivered me. I'm not a child abuser any longer. I am free," I whispered.

Tears trickled down my cheeks and I hugged Mark tighter, kissing his head. "Thank you, Jesus. Thank you. I'm so grateful. I love you so much. Thank you for loving me during this past year when I didn't deserve it. Of course, when will I ever deserve it, right?"

Without realizing it, an old hymn formed on my lips, even though my throat closed as I tried not to sob. "Turn your eyes upon Jesus, look full in his wonderful face. And the things of earth will grow strangely dim in the light of his glory and grace."

Oh Jesus, yes, your glory and grace wipe out all the pain and sorrow of this year. You've touched me. I love you.

Many songs filled my mind as my joy sought expression. Mark was asleep but I wasn't concerned I might wake him. I wanted to wake the whole world. *I want everyone to know: Jesus is in control of my life.*

The next couple of days were filled with shopping, baking, and sending out Christmas cards. Christmas was approaching all too fast. Christmas dinner at my home for ten family members was foremost in my thoughts and plans. I hadn't had time to even think about the board's Christmas party.

Then one day Larry mentioned, "You'll never guess what my supervisor told me last night. I have too many vacation hours on the books and have to take some time off before the new year otherwise I lose them completely. Isn't that wild?"

I jerked my head towards him. "Honey," I exclaimed, "that's the answer to my prayer. Now you can go to the board Christmas party. Can you ask for next Tuesday, the twentieth, off?"

He smiled. "Yeah, that's right. That's great. Sure I can. Now, they'll have to let me have it off."

I could barely sit still as I grinned at him. *Thank you, Jesus, you did it. I trusted you and you did it.*

Larry's smile grew as I hugged him. "Kathy, the Lord has answered your prayer. I wasn't sure he could do it but he did."

My excitement grew through the week after Larry confirmed he could have the night off.

On Tuesday evening, we arrived at the fancy restaurant of a local hotel. I was truly grateful Larry was beside me as we ate the delicious food and enjoyed the special entertainment.

Five days later on Christmas morning, Darcy woke us early as expected. She was so excited about seeing what Santa Claus had brought her. Instructing her to stay in her room, Larry, my mother, and I turned on the Christmas tree lights and made sure the camera was ready to capture her delight as she saw her gifts for the first time. I opened the drapes. The dawn's soft pink light filtered into the room creating a fairyland effect on the presents. The blinking tree lights cast red, blue, and orange shadows on the walls and my spirit was illuminated with hope and joy.

Christmas morning ... the day we celebrate our Savior's birth and the first step in his journey for our salvation. And this was the morning of the birth of a life free from hurting Darcy, free from uncontrolled anger, free from condemnation and hate. As a cocoon opens to reveal a ready-to-fly butterfly, my life was opening also to love, faith, and patience. Christmas morning ... God's gift of Jesus and God's gift of abundant life for me and my family.

UPDATE

July 2017

Chapter 20 occurred at Christmas, 1977. I've shared my story over five hundred times at speaking engagements and through articles, and referred to it in various aspects in my books. Yet at times, I'm still brought to tears when I focus on the pain I brought to my family, especially to Darcy, my precious daughter, a gift from God. I cringe facing the reality of how she, as an unprotected child, must have felt. Her confusion and fear seem even more real to me. Now, as a lay counselor, I've heard the stories from adults who tell of that kind of childhood and it breaks my heart. And to think I was one of those abusive parents breaks it twice-fold.

When I struggled, little was known about what is now called postpartum depression, or "baby blues." Although I suspect I was affected by that, I have no way of knowing for sure. Because of my shame and feeling like I was alone in my battle, I didn't consult a doctor, fearing the contempt of even him. But the hormonal imbalance after giving birth is real, and if you struggle like I did, I urge you to consult a doctor. Medicine can help restore any chemical imbalances within your body enabling you to correctly deal with any other issues affecting your reactions. Often those physical problems exaggerate sinful patterns, like perfectionism. Those underlying emotional and mental causes will still need to be dealt with, but at least you'll have fewer impacting issues to resolve.

In spite of the possible physical influences, God in his gracious love knew the plan for restoration of our family. He empowered Darcy to forgive me for the pain I inflicted on her. God's gift of enabling her to allow God to use our story for his glory began as early as when she was in fifth grade and this story was first published in book form. She said, "Mom, I'm so excited you're an author, I want to take your book to school with me and show it to my teacher."

I was surprised and felt embarrassed thinking of her showing her teacher. Darcy knew the book was about our story and how I treated her. She couldn't remember details, other than what I told her. Yet, she still wanted to show it to others.

Of course, I agreed. A few months later, Darcy returned with the book and said her teacher and many teachers and the principal from her public school had read it. As I took the book from her, I noticed there was a note attached. It was from her teacher and read, "Mrs. Miller: I really love your daughter. She is a happy, well-adjusted little girl."

I began crying, trying not to sob. The fears I had of Darcy being psychologically and emotionally ruined forever were unfounded. Her teacher had confirmed it.

I also had feared she could never possibly want a relationship with me, yet today, we are very close. In fact, she calls me her best friend. She has always wanted God glorified through the telling of our story. She loves God and seeks him as she is now a loving wife and mother of two. She and I wrote a book about mother and daughter relationships and she is a budding novelist.

Larry and I are also close to our son Mark who didn't seem affected by the chaos since he was less than two years old when peace was restored.

And yes, Larry and I experience a wonderful and wonder-filled joyful marriage far beyond what I could ever have imagined or desired. We are not only best friends; our passion is to see God glorified through our lives and ministry. We are on the "same page" of purpose and mission. We co-author books together, speak often together, and give soul care counseling to many.

My desire is you will have ever greater trust and hope in God regardless of your temptations, challenges, and failures. God is indeed the God of everlasting love and mercy. There is always hope with such a great God.

If you are reading this and have never encountered this loving God as one who saw your need for rescue from your sin and sent his most precious Son Jesus to die for you on Calvary's cross, you can tell him you need him as your only source of being saved. Whether your sin is like mine--uncontrolled anger, bitterness, and discontent--or something seemingly less destructive, you indeed have sinned. Only God is perfect. Face your need of a Savior and confess your sin and submit to him. He is calling to you and wants to redeem you and become the Lord of your life. You'll still have many challenges, but you'll have his power for this earthly life and you'll enjoy his presence in heaven.

I'd love to hear from you through my website's contact form: www.KathyCollardMiller.com.

MESSAGE FROM LARRY

Although I know now I wounded Kathy in many ways because of my selfishness, I can say honestly, I never purposefully and willfully intended to harm her. I actually wanted to love her but I didn't how to do that. I'm not defending my actions. I was wrong. I sinned against God and against Kathy. But now I know why I reacted the sinful way I did. It wasn't *against* Kathy as much as it was *for* me.

In my own immaturity and rejection of God's plan for being a loving husband and father, I found value in other things like working and having a flying hobby which I could "conquer" and feel good at. It was easy to rationalize my choices because it seemed like nothing I did was good enough for Kathy. I concluded I could never please her so why even try. Even when I did try to do things for Kathy and the family, there was always something I didn't do, or I did poorly, in her mind, negating my effort. In fact, I truly thought I was loving them the best I could by working toward our financial security.

These are not excuses. I know now I wasn't trusting God. I chose to fulfill my needs selfishly at the expense of Kathy and my children.

Kathy was right. I did have a "mistress." It wasn't another woman, it was what I "worshipped": what I depended upon to make me feel strong and important. My choices disregarded God. I believed my job, flying, real estate success, and not having children would meet my needs.

The primary turning point occurred when Kathy released trying to make me provide everything she needed. When she made a very scary and difficult choice to think "I love you." Although I didn't know what she had done, I noticed a difference in her and the way she responded to me. She was more considerate of my needs and didn't hound me when I didn't do what she wanted. She was cheerful and greeted me at the door. When I did the smallest thing, she expressed her gratitude instead of waiting until I fulfilled every aspect of what she wanted.

Since the pressure to be her "everything" was no longer there, I didn't feel like I needed to run from her. I could move toward her emotionally and physically. I didn't have to face being something I knew intrinsically I had no ability providing.

I'm so very grateful Kathy obeyed God in making the choice to love me, even though she didn't feel love for me at all. Her obedience started the process of my heart being softened.

I've asked God, Kathy, Darcy, and Mark to forgive me and they graciously have. I'm very grateful. My passion now is to make God look good through worshipping him and believing he can meet my needs. I want to love Kathy, my children and my grandchildren with God's kind of love. I still am challenged to do that but God is making inroads.

Today, I'm very happy with my life, marriage, and family. I know it's God's work in my heart to want to make them a priority. Kathy is now the highest human priority to me and we can freely serve God together because we have the same goals: to glorify God in whatever way he desires. Of course, our relationship isn't perfect. We often disagree and have different ideas of how to work through challenges and disagreements. But the difference is we both no longer feel accused and threatened by each other. We are united, on the same team. And as a result, we both seek God to help us.

We both believe there is hope for any hurting marriage and family. God is powerful enough and we are living testimonies of God's work. Together, we give God the glory and praise.

—Larry Miller

INDIVIDUAL AND GROUP DISCUSSION QUESTIONS

Chapter 1 Anger Controlled Me

1. How did you feel anticipating reading this book?

2. What drew you to read it?

3. Overall, what is your opinion and/or feelings about someone who abuses children?

4. What kind of beliefs or ideas seemed to feed the author's anger?

5. How can you tell the foundation for anger has already been set?

6. What do you think the author believed Darcy was communicating through disobedience?

7. Why do you think Christians think other Christians could never be child abusers?

8. Why do you think someone believes they must deny they struggle or are sinning?

9. How can the expectations of being a perfect mother contribute to frustration?

10. What connection did the author link between God's presence and his help? Is that a wise and/or accurate conclusion?

Chapter 2 Promises! Promises!

1. Can you identify with the author's desire to get away from home "out in the real world all by myself"?

2. Why does being out in the "real world" become so important to mothers?

3. How can clothing become a boost for a woman's spirits? In what ways is that wise and unwise?

4. How does the author feel "voiceless"? What do you think the "message" about her would seem to be? I.e.: unimportant, etc.

5. What do you feel like when your words are not heard, dismissed, or debated? How do you handle that?

6. Do you think it's unusual someone would want someone else to die? How did you feel reading the author's prayer for her husband to die?

7. How does a wife begin to believe her husband must meet her needs in order for her to be who God wants her to be?

8. How could the author have taken advantage of Larry's question, "How come you're going to bed so early?"

9. What are some possible reasons Jill responded the way she did?

10. Although "praying more" is always a good idea, in this case, why do you think it was ineffective?

Chapter 3 In Training

1. What does "What am I doing wrong? She's never going to learn" indicate about the author's beliefs and fears? Do you think they're founded?

2. What other beliefs and fears does the author believe about Darcy and herself?

3. How does wanting people to believe the best about us keep us in our sinful reactions?

4. How is Christian fellowship and community supposed to help us get out of our sinful reactions?

5. Why do parents tend to blame themselves for their child's misbehavior? How do you fight that wrong idea?

6. To what degree do you think children are motivated by a parent's urging? To what degree does a child's ability to control themselves influence a child's obedience?

7. List the ways the author believes Darcy has potty training accidents on purpose.

8. If you've believe(d) that, share why.

9. Do you think a parent is responsible to make a child happy?

10. How does the desire for perfection bring frustration or unhappiness in parenting?

Chapter 4 Never On Top

1. How does a lack of sleep affect the ability to be a good mother?

2. What have you found to help when you are sleep-deprived?

3. How do expectations set someone up to become angry?

4. Is there a particular area of expectations producing anger more often? When you are successful resisting temptation, what helps?

5. Why do we sometimes react to a child's accidental mistakes as though they were intentional?

6. Why is it hard to see accidents as accidents?

7. When we rehearse our dissatisfaction or discontent, what do we think it will gain us?

8. What lies about who God is contribute to us believing God is punishing us when things go badly or expectations are unfulfilled?

9. What might we believe about ourselves when God doesn't answer a prayer for an instantaneous deliverance of our anger or another sinful pattern?

10. Why are mothers reluctant to take needed naps? Have you found a way to convince yourself to take a nap?

11. Do you think a joyful attitude increases energy—and the opposite? Why or why not?

12. What verse would help you right now in whatever challenges you are facing?

13. How can thinking, "I'll never get angry again" set a mother up for failure?

Chapter 5 Trusting

1. When something is important to you, how can prayer become more like demanding?

2. What does demanding something from God look or sound like?

3. Do you think the author was requesting or demanding in wanting to go to her in-law's home?

4. What do you think of when you read "ambivalence"? How would you define it?

5. Have you experienced the ambivalence of opposing feelings like love and dislike? Describe.

6. What do you brood about most often as a mom?

7. If your child whines, how do you handle it? What do you find yourself whining about—if you do?

8. Can you share an example of God's unexpected provision?

9. When you've reacted poorly with your child, how do you respond and deal with the guilt?

10. How do you counteract remembering the times when God didn't seem to answer your prayers the way you'd like?

11. What Scripture(s) build a wall of faith for you?

Chapter 6 Bittersweet

1. What is the most difficult challenge you face in your marriage?

2. How could the author have expressed her tension about Larry not paying the bills?

3. What does the author seem to believe about how patience and contentment are gained?

4. When you are unhappy, what do you use to escape and feel better?

5. Is it easy or hard for you to say "no" to an opportunity which you would enjoy, but it's not God's timing?

6. Have you ever seen your child(ren) as blocks to doing God's will?

7. Does mothering sometimes feel like a trap?

8. The author tells Darcy "we won't go for any more walks." Do you sometimes use the extreme degree of a consequence to motivate your child? What is the disadvantage of that? What is a better choice?

9. What circumstances bring on depression and/or hopelessness most often for you?

Chapter 7 Five Gallons

1. When "warning bells" go off in your thinking, what most often causes you to ignore them?

2. Why do you think moms often expect their child to obey even when it's an unrealistic expectation?

3. The author often belittles Darcy verbally with accusations and name calling. Why does verbally belittling seem productive or useful at times? How do you resist that lie?

4. The author says, "I don't hate her. I hate myself." How can such a realization be helpful?

5. Does any kind of eating pattern contribute to your lack of self-control toward your children or others?

6. God uses the water bottle breakage to get the author's attention. Has God used anything to draw your attention to a needed change?

7. Do you ever wonder what your children will say about you when they are grown? What is your greatest fear? What do you want them to say?

Chapter 8 Big Difference

1. How do you resist the temptation to make your plans more important than your children?

2. Since children aren't the only thing a woman takes care of, how do you make choices for responding to their perceived needs, like playing a game?

3. Is it always selfishness for a mother to choose time for herself? How do you determine such a choice?

4. How can a mother keep her promises to her child like, "I'll play the game more often"? What do you think the specific, realistic promise should be?

5. How could the author have dealt better with the disappointment of a cancelled RSVP so it doesn't affect her patience level?

6. Why does it seem reasonable to expect a mother's anger to motivate a child to obey?

7. Why is a child not motivated to obey when a parent is angry?

8. Why do you think it is so important for the author to be ready for the party?

9. What expectations do you struggle with when you try to get things done? What seems threatened if you don't succeed in all your plans?

10. At times, a wife and mom can think, "I got him to the altar and now I'll alter him." Has that been your attitude to any degree?

11. If you've thought cleaning the house or any other activity is more fulfilling than giving your children the attention they need, what do you attribute it to?

12. Do you consider yourself very consistent in giving consequences? How could you increase your consistency?

13. The author changes her wording from "you did it again" to "the next time." What change of thinking does that indicate? Why do you think it might have a positive effect in the child?

14. How do you feel about spanking? It's a controversial topic. Although the author believes it can be used correctly, if you disagree, what consequences instead could you use for a toddler?

Chapter 9 Can't Say No

1. To what degree do you struggle with saying "no"? For what activities or relationships do you feel obligated to always say "yes"?

2. What does saying "yes" provide for you? Does God want to provide that for you in some other way? Does always saying "yes" leave him out in some way?

3. What did you think and feel when you read, "An opportunity is not necessarily God's open door"? Do you agree or disagree? Explain.

4. If the statement seems correct, what are the obstacles to living it out?

5. Other than the ideas the author had, can you think of other reasons the sentence could be true and beneficial?

Chapter 10 Suicide

1. If your husband doesn't respond as you'd like—or anyone else close to you—do you displace your anger from him onto anyone else? if so, what does that look like?

2. How easy is it for you to blame someone else for your reactions?

3. Why do you think humans tend to do that?

4. If you were the author's friend, what would you say to her?

5. If you are struggling with anger or any other ungodly reaction, what do you want to hear from a friend or from God?

6. Have you ever considered suicide? If so, what happened?

7. Have you ever helped someone dealing with suicidal thoughts? Even if you haven't, what do you think a friend should tell a suicidal friend?

8. When we fear someone knowing the real "me," what are the ways we might block being known?

9. What is the thing about you that you fear most people knowing? How do you protect yourself from being seen like that?

10. What does it seem would happen if a person knew the real you?

Chapter 11 Confession

1. Have you ever felt as paranoid as the author? If so, can you describe your feelings and thoughts?

2. Why do you think it's so easy to compare our lives to others?

3. When you are tempted to do that, how do you battle it?

4. Why do you think seeing someone's ordered home makes us think their house is always like that?

5. How can Christians or any group of friends help each other with their problems—whether it's anger or something else?

6. How has fear of someone's negative reaction prevented you from sharing?

7. What physical reactions indicate you are starting to become angry?

8. Does it make sense anger creates energy? What do you do with that energy?

9. Have you ever noticed you can't identify the real reason of your frustration? How do you handle it when you have recognized the real, underlying cause?

10. Can you share an example of anger being caused by a lack of trust in God?

11. Can you share a time when turning your heart and mind to trusting God made a difference in empowering patience and understanding toward others?

12. What happened when you tried to ask for prayer about a personal struggle?

13. Is James 5:16 meaningful to you in any way?

Chapter 12 Celebrate!

1. Is it easy or difficult to accept whatever level of love or acceptance a significant person in your life can give you?

2. What do you think has blocked you, if applicable? What do you think other women might find as blocks to satisfaction?

3. What are you seeing in the author and her husband's anniversary dinner contributing to their difficulties? Can you relate to any of that?

4. How did the author's demand of enjoying an uneventful party contribute to her tension and temptation?

5. What have you seen or think nagging does to the other person?

6. What is the author hoping to gain from nagging?

7. How do you describe unconditional love? What advice would you give the author for reaching such a goal?

8. How do you think the author is trying to manipulate her husband to love her?

9. If you'd heard God's message "show your love," how would you have thought to follow through?

10. Why can we be convinced other people love the same things we do.

Chapter 13 Surprise Party

1. What is your reaction to the author's plan?

2. Have you ever done something with the purpose of making someone love you more?

3. Do you think children can sense the tension of others? If so, to what degree do you think it influences their behavior?

4. In her haste, the author left the clay on the table where Darcy could get to it. She inadvertently set up the situation she was trying to avoid. How can a parent stay strong under these circumstances?

5. Why do you think the author thinks the party must be perfect? What might seem dangerous if it isn't? Or what might she lose?

6. How is the author forgetting about God?

7. Why do you think the author believes rehearsing "you made a mess" will serve some good purpose? What would the purpose be?

8. Do you think it does any good to apologize to a child who can't understand the concept? If there is good, what would it be?

Chapter 14 Love Is...

1. The author uses the word "always" which seems to confirm the hopelessness she feels. How does thinking in terms of "this always happens…" "he always does that…" or other "all or nothing" statements contribute to discontent and unhealthy relationships?

2. How is a phrase like "from then on" a kind of "all or nothing" statement?

3. Why does it seem incongruent to love and dislike/hate at the same time or close together?

4. Do you think it's real love if it exists alongside feelings of hate or dislike?

5. Do you agree "love is a choice, not a feeling"? Support your belief with Scripture or other ideas.

6. Why does feeling the incongruence of love and hate seem to negate or discount when we've treated someone lovingly?

7. How could making a list about the level of your child's development help you in specific ways?

8. Can you share an example of lowering your frustration level by diminishing your expectations?

9. If the potty training of your child is challenging, what do you think you should do?

10. What was your reaction to the struggle for the author to say or think "I love you"? Is there anyone you need to make a choice to love by thinking "I love you"?

Chapter 15 Seven Steps

Note: The book by Tim LaHaye, *Understanding the Male Temperament*, is now out of print.

1. Are you familiar with the concept of temperaments? They are many different ways the concepts are taught. Share whatever you know about those ideas.

2. If you know about them, why do you think they're helpful?

3. To what degree do you see yourself as a perfectionist?

4. If you see perfectionistic tendencies in your life, describe how they are revealed.

5. What do you think would help a perfectionist release perfectionistic kind of thinking and acting?

6. Of the seven steps covered in Tim LaHaye's book, which is most important for you?

7. Which of the seven steps is hardest for you to implement?

8. Which of the choices or ideas the author newly understands helps you the most?

9. What are more reasons Christians think God wants them to have an instantaneous deliverance of their ungodly reactions?

10. For whatever you struggle with, write out verses referring to the problem and put them throughout the house.

11. To what degree do you consider someone else responsible for your happiness? What would you like to do about it?

Chapter 16 Victory in Sight

1. What is your reaction about step five: "give thanks for anything that bothers you"?

2. Why do you think the author feels helpless when someone calls and wants to talk? Why do you think she's can't excuse herself? What would you do in that situation?

3. The author is particularly sensitive to being seen as dependable. If you could talk to the author about that, what would you say? Is there something about yourself you want people to recognize or not acknowledge?

4. If you've begun applying the seven steps from Tim LaHaye's book, what has happened? Has there been any effect?

5. What happens within a mom when she thinks she's the only one struggling with anger?

6. How does Satan use the guilt and condemnation of thinking she's the only one that bad?

7. Why do women in a group, especially a church group, tend to not talk about their struggles?

8. What do you think makes it possible for a group to honestly share their struggles?

9. Is it easy or hard for you to acknowledge God's provision when you make loving choices toward your children?

Chapter 17 Loved

1. What do you think about the author's assessment she doesn't qualify to serve on the board? What is your opinion about how "mature" a Christian needs to be to serve others?

2. What would you have thought when the second call came to take the position?

3. The circumstances in the author's life seem to affirm the decision to join the board. When is it unwise to only go by circumstances in seeking God's will?

4. How did you feel reading the author's awareness of God's work which showed his love for her?

5. Have you ever experienced such an awareness, especially during or after struggling with a continuing ungodly reaction?

6. Why do you think the author was surprised at the feelings of love she had for God?

7. Although we shouldn't judge our love for God on our feelings, how can the feelings draw us closer to him, even empowering us to respond with more godly responses?

8. What was your reaction, feelings and thoughts, about how God led the author to make changes in her own life and how the change in her affected Larry's feelings toward her?

9. If someone reads this who doesn't end up with similar results, what would you say to her?

10. In your own life, are you afraid your wise choices won't bring you the results you want? What could that indicate about your motives of making the wise choices?

Chapter 18 Not Perfect Yet

1. How can feeling too confident about God's work sometimes set someone up for failure? Has that happened to you? What is a healthy perspective?

2. At the same time, is it wrong to enjoy the results of God's work? What would you say to someone who fears enjoying it too much and wonders if it will continue.

3. Sometimes fear results because of the expectation we'll feel like a fool if we trust and then are rejected or defeated again. How would you respond to such a possibility?

4. When do you most often feel tempted to let go of your commitment to faithfully give consequences to your child for misbehavior?

5. Do you think it was too early or unrealistic for the author to expect even a month of no outbursts to mean she was over her anger habit entirely?

6. What was your reaction to a wooden spoon being used? If you don't like that idea, and yet want to spank, what would you choose to do?

7. The author is not advocating spanking as the only disciplinary option but it did work for her. Do you agree or disagree with her? How would you share your disagreement with her?

8. Do you think it's possible to give a spanking without anger? Why or why not?

9. The author seems to persist in putting a lot of expectations upon herself. How do you think she healthfully responded this time?

10. What do you think of her thought, "No one will care or even know what isn't done?" Does that seem true to you or not?

11. To what degree do you believe your husband or another significant person to you should read your mind? How do you deal with that?

Chapter 19 Forgiven

1. The author shares some very vulnerable thoughts as she examines her heart. What was your reaction to her thinking?

2. Have you ever felt like the author? If so, have you ever shared them with someone? If not, what do you fear could happen?

3. If you have shared similar feelings with others, what prompted you and how did it feel? What were the reactions of others?

4. How does not sharing, especially what seems like shameful thoughts, become a hindrance to walking close to God or others? How does it affect the reactions of a mother toward her child?

5. Have you experienced mothering as something requiring more than you can give? How have you become aware of those thoughts?

6. Exactly what is it that mothering requires which can feel overwhelming?

7. How have you dealt with those overwhelmed feelings?

8. After feeling frustrated with your child, does it seem to connect with thinking you don't love her or him? Or does it seem the two are not related?

9. When does it seem your child isn't God's special gift?

Chapter 20 In Control

1. How do you coordinate what could seem opposing ideas: bad things happening and yet God is seen working?

2. What do you think the author's growing trust in God, specifically for the Christmas party, is based on?

3. Can you share a time when you were surprisingly calm and trusting God about something you really wanted—yet it looked almost impossible?

4. Did you relate to the author's joyful reverie in the middle of the night? When have you experienced that?

5. The author talks about not deserving God's love, even though she's responding better. Do you think someone ever deserves God's love? Explain your answer.

6. What did you think about Larry being able to have the time off to go to the board Christmas party?

7. Do you have an answer to prayer similar or something you'd like to share?

8. Having read the book, what is your overall reaction?

9. What is the most important idea you want to remember?

10. What is the most important truth you want to implement?

ABOUT THE AUTHOR

Kathy Collard Miller's writing and speaking ministry began after God delivered her from being a child abuser, as recounted in this book. After she realized God had indeed healed her and her family, she attended a community writing class where she learned how to submit article ideas to magazines. She sent the idea of telling her story to *Moody Monthly Magazine* with the stipulation it be published anonymously. She was still so ashamed she couldn't bear the thought of other people knowing what she had done. The editors wanted the article and agreed to it being anonymous. It was published in 1978.

When Kathy received the news of the acceptance, she was very excited and began telling others about her first article being accepted. She didn't realize their next question would be, "What is the article about?" As a result, she had to begin confessing what had happened. Thankfully no one reacted with shock or condemnation which gave her confidence in sharing. In fact, the response usually built the faith of the other person. This encouraged Kathy to continue sharing.

When Kathy told a woman at her church about God's work in her life and family, the woman responded, "You should tell your story to our young mom's group. I'm going to tell our leader." Kathy replied, "Oh no, I have no intention of ever sharing." The woman did tell the group's leader and by the time she invited Kathy to share, God had changed Kathy's heart to be willing to reveal her sin.

At that first speaking opportunity in 1980, Kathy realized the value of sharing her story which gave glory to God. The responses of the one hundred twenty women demonstrated to Kathy God could use her story. Her presentation had given hope to many young moms and built their faith in God's power.

When Kathy was invited to speak at other churches, she was ready. As a result, over the years, she has spoken in more than thirty US states and eight foreign countries. She speaks on a variety of topics including trusting God, parenting, marriage, security in Christ, inheritance in Christ, perfectionism, women of the Bible, knowing God in truth, among others. Kathy loves to make the Bible come alive and applicable for every woman. She uses humor and practical ideas based in a biblical foundation.

In the same year of her first speaking engagement, 1980, Kathy attended her first writers conference and then the story in this book was published as *Out of Control* in 1984. Her writing ministry expanded and she now has more than fifty books published including women's Bible studies, Bible commentaries, Christian Living topics, and compiled books. She has more than three hundred published articles and more than seven hundred posts on her blog.

Kathy's first television appearance was on *The 700 Club* as she told her story, shortly before *Out of Control* was published. Since then she has been on numerous television programs and hundreds of radio programs.

Larry and Kathy continue to write and speak together and reach out to others as lay counselors, plus being active in the leadership of their church. They live in Southern California near Palm Springs. They are parents to two and grandparents to two. Reach them at www.KathyCollardMiller.com.

BOOKS BY KATHY COLLARD MILLER WITH ELK LAKE PUBLISHING, INC.

Pure-Hearted: The Blessings of Living Out God's Glory
Daughters of the King Bible study series:
Choices of the Heart: ten lessons about the women of the Bible, contrasting two different women of the Bible about different topics.
Whispers of My Heart: ten lessons about prayer.

Coming soon:
At the Heart of Friendship: ten lessons about different aspects of relationships.
Heart Wisdom: ten lessons about different topics covered in the biblical book of Proverbs.

www.ingramcontent.com/pod-product-compliance
Lightning Source LLC
LaVergne TN
LVHW051056080426
835508LV00019B/1914